ADVANCE PRAISE

"My wife and I feel fortunate to have met Bill over twenty years ago, benefiting from his personalized counsel ever since. Throughout my executive career, transitioning into a Section 16 officer role and eventually into retirement, his advice on matters extending beyond traditional financial concerns has been thoughtful, caring, and insightful. Readers can learn much from his perspectives on work, health, and life balance."

—FRANK LITTLE, RETIRED EXECUTIVE
VICE PRESIDENT OF 3M COMPANY

"I met Bill shortly after he lost 100+ pounds. It's not often you meet someone who understands that ideal body weight is only step one in the process of increasing your lifespan and healthspan. Bill takes a proactive approach, and that is exactly what is required for any C-suite executive to live a life free from the effects of aging. Bill does a great job outlining the synergistic relationship between wealth and health and how he was able to reverse his own biological age."

—SHAWN TOLLESON, FOUNDER OF TOLLESON
HEALTH ADVISORS, FORMER MLB PITCHER

"I have known Bill Burns for over twenty years, and he has provided me with exceptional financial planning advice as I climbed the corporate ladder. During that time, we both gained considerable weight as we dealt with the stresses of our respective jobs. I watched as Bill lost 124 pounds over 294 days and, most impressively, kept it off for more than five years. He inspired me on my own weight loss journey. In Section 16 Secrets, Bill provides an easy-to-understand path to assist all corporate officers who want to better navigate their wealth, and more important, their health."

—TONY TRIPENY, RETIRED EXECUTIVE VICE PRESIDENT AND CHIEF FINANCIAL OFFICER OF CORNING INCORPORATED

"Section 16 officers are the highest paid employees in their companies, but what good are financial rewards if the pressure of their job takes years off their life? Bill Burns presents a different mindset—use your wealth to buy back your health—and shows that by investing just 1 percent of their net worth into their health on an annual basis, they could add a significant number of years to their healthspan. This is a guide for corporate officers who would like to extend their healthy years on the planet."

—DAN SULLIVAN, CO-FOUNDER & PRESIDENT OF STRATEGIC COACH®. BESTSELLING CO-AUTHOR OF WHO NOT HOW AND THE GAP AND THE GAIN

"I've worked with Bill over the last several years to optimize his longevity, health, and performance. Bill has come to understand that money is not an asset. Money is a resource. Health, quality relationships, and a greater sense of purpose are assets. Any time we can invest a resource to protect assets it is the best investment we can make. Kudos to Bill for figuring this out and wanting to share it with the world!"

—JEFFREY R. GLADDEN, MD, FACC, FOUNDER & CEO OF GLADDEN LONGEVITY

SECTION 16 SECRETS

SECTION

16

SECRETS

How Corporate Insiders
Amplify Wealth & Buy Back Health

WILLIAM B. BURNS, JR. CFP®

LIONCREST
PUBLISHING

SECTION 16 SECRETS

How Corporate Insiders Amplify Wealth & Buy Back Health

FIRST EDITION

ISBN   978-1-5445-4030-6   *Hardcover*
       978-1-5445-4029-0   *Paperback*
       978-1-5445-4031-3   *Ebook*

To my family—Donna, Billy, Shannon, Matt,
Nate, Catherine, and Braeden.

Thank you for your love and understanding during
the writing process over the past three years.

Thank you for supporting my quest to live until 105, and I look forward
to seeing you all at Braeden's 50th high school jubilee in 2073.

CONTENTS

NOTE TO THE READER

All names and companies have been changed for privacy purposes.

Section 16 officers are not allowed to implement all the strategies we will review. The Securities and Exchange Commission (SEC) requires all publicly traded companies to disclose if they allow executives to utilize hedging transactions to reduce their risk of loss. Many companies have chosen to prohibit their officers from using some (or all) of these hedging strategies. The rationale is that the financial fortunes of Section 16 officers need to be tied directly to the company's performance. Any method that reduces the risk of loss decreases the correlation to company performance. A Section 16 officer must check with their corporate counsel before implementing any of the strategies outlined in *Section 16 Secrets*.

Although I have personally benefited from the various health products and devices referenced in *Section 16 Secrets*, it is important to disclose that any statements related to these products have not been evaluated by the Food and Drug Administration (FDA), and these products are not intended to diagnose, treat, cure, or prevent any disease.

I will be referencing physiological and medical data; however, I am not a medical professional, so nothing in *Section 16 Secrets* should be construed as medical advice. For example, although fasting is considered safe for most people, in some cases, you should not attempt to fast for either physiological or psychological reasons. I will provide references where applicable so you can conduct independent research. It is crucial you meet with your personal physician before undertaking any change in activity, exercise, or diet.

Finally, the insurance information contained within *Section 16 Secrets* is for illustrative purposes only. I am not an insurance agent. Please review your personal needs with your insurance agent licensed in your state of residency.

INTRODUCTION

"It is health that is real wealth and not pieces of gold and silver."

—MAHATMA GANDHI

From 2007 to 2017, I lost a decade of a healthy life.

During the financial crisis of 2007–2009, my workload increased significantly. I was eating more fast food, and exercise was nonexistent. Gaining ten pounds in a year does not sound like a lot until you add it up over a decade. By 2017, I weighed 309 pounds.

I found myself in the same position as the Section 16 officers and corporate insiders I've worked with for over twenty-three years. In a profession that sometimes requires 24/7 client attention, I often work long hours. When you leave the office at 10:00 p.m., you are not thinking about eating healthy, and you certainly do not plan to stop at the gym on the way home. It almost always seemed like there were not enough hours in the day.

Section 16 officers and corporate insiders work harder than most to climb the corporate ladder, only to sacrifice their health along the way. The hours they log in a high-stress position (along with a poor diet and lack of exercise) can take years off their lives.

Does any of this sound familiar?

What if I told you there was a way to "buy back" some of the health you lost—that you can increase your lifespan (the total number of years you live) and your healthspan (the number of years spent in generally good health, without any chronic disease or disabilities typically associated with aging) as well? What would an extra decade (or two) of quality living be worth to you? Would you invest $5,000 a year if it produced extra, high-caliber years? What about $50,000 or $100,000?

I want to be around for my children, grandchildren, and great-grandchildren, but when I weighed 309 pounds, that seemed improbable. So in 2017, I decided to correct the path I was on. I hired a personal trainer who guided me along a weight-loss journey where I shed 124 pounds in 294 days, and I have kept the weight off in the five years since. Then in 2019, I invested in a relationship with a longevity physician, a concierge medical professional who asked me, "How good do you want to be?" My longevity physician is helping me look decades in the future and get in front of potential problems today—not waiting until I am "sick." My investment in these two relationships likely added two decades (or more) to my life. I want to share what I have learned with others.

WHAT IS SECTION 16?

I remember when I got the call from Tom, a close friend of a long-term client. Tom works for Silica-Corp, a Fortune 500 company, and was recently promoted to executive vice president of manufacturing. As part of his orientation, he learned he is now considered a Section 16 officer—a corporate insider.

Section 16 refers to the part of the Securities and Exchange Act of 1934 that governs the regulatory filing responsibilities for directors, officers, and 10 percent shareholders of publicly traded companies. This rule also applies to family members of these directors, officers, and 10 percent shareholders, referred to as beneficial owners. (More on this later.)

The purpose of the Section 16 filing requirements is transparency—for insiders to disclose their initial equity position in the company and then update the public on how their equity holdings change over time, from their purchases and sales of company stock.

Tom has been with his organization for over twenty years and has accumulated a net worth of approximately $6 million. He has been a saver all his life, and excluding his mortgage, he has no debt.

He and Sarah are both 55 and have five children, whom they enjoy traveling with when time allows. Tom has been fortunate to provide for those vacations out of his current salary, without skimping on his 401(k) contributions or other savings. Ranging from age 13 to 20, two of Tom and Sarah's children attend college; their youngest child is in eighth grade; and the other two children at home are both in high school, one is a sophomore and the other a junior. He and his wife are proud of the fact that their college-age children can go to school without any student loans (Tom and Sarah were early contributors to 529 college savings plans).

As a Section 16 officer, Tom must adhere to the Section 16 filing requirements. He knows he has to fill out some paperwork and turn it in somewhere, but he is brand new to the process and does not know where to start.

SECTION 16 GPS™ AND HEALTHSPAN EXTENDER™

Tom and Sarah need help navigating their new Section 16 world. In Part 1 of *Section 16 Secrets*, we will first follow their journey through the *Section 16 GPS* process. The process includes a set of financial planning and investment strategies to navigate corporate insiders' compensation programs and help them start thinking about the bigger world around them. Time is a valuable commodity for Section 16 officers. Just like the GPS in your car will get you to your destination quickly and more efficiently, so will the *Section 16 GPS* process. Its aim is to help Section 16 officers *amplify* their wealth.

The *Section 16 GPS* process focuses on three main elements:

- Guidance: Employee options and restricted shares, trading windows, and the need for diversification.
- Philanthropy: Tax-advantaged gifts and impact giving. Impact giving helps donors forge a closer relationship with the charities they support, working toward predefined and measurable goals.
- Stewardship: Identify ways to pass on your core family

values, in addition to your financial assets, to the next generation.

Once you have the *Section 16 GPS* process down, we will review the importance of retiring "to" something and not "from" something. Then we will work to frame the second half of your life, by helping you improve your lifespan *and* healthspan. In Part 2 of *Section 16 Secrets*, we will review *The Healthspan Extender*, a mindset to extend your longevity and buy back some of the health you may have lost climbing the corporate ladder. We will examine the benefits of genetic testing, longevity physicians, and how to improve your biological age.

DO YOU WANT TO TURN BACK THE CLOCK OF AGING?

When I think of my parents, it makes me sad to reflect on their missed milestones. My mother passed away at 43 from a brain aneurysm no one knew she had. She missed every high school and college graduation for my two sisters and me and could not attend our weddings. She never felt the joy of holding her grandchildren.

It also makes me sad knowing my dad missed witnessing his grandchildren's high school and college athletic achievements. At six feet five inches tall, he was an exceptional basketball and baseball player in high school and college but didn't get to see those same skills in his grandchildren. He never saw Billy's progression from a seventh-grade "C" team basketball player to varsity starter to college player. He missed Matthew's basketball travels across the country with our Amateur Athletic Union (AAU) team. He never felt both the nervousness and exhilaration of seeing Nathan take the mound as a collegiate baseball pitcher. His granddaughter Catherine is the toughest of the bunch and, as a three-sport athlete, received multiple accolades he would have been very proud of. Catherine was named to all-state teams for both softball and soccer her senior year. He never got a chance to meet Braeden. My dad died about three months before he was born. To see Braeden dunking on the basketball court at age 16 would have brought a smile to his face.

My father passed away at 67 from pulmonary hypertension (high blood pressure within the arteries of the lungs). It is a rare disease, with only a small number of new cases reported each year. He attended our graduations, two out of three weddings, and met four of his ten grandchildren, but he missed everything else.

It is not only my parents who missed out. I often think about the knowledge, wisdom, family history, and stories my parents could have passed along to my children. I wish they could have had a relationship with my parents as they transitioned into adulthood.

I have worked with Section 16 executives and corporate insiders for more than twenty-three years and have learned a lot about life, loss, and shared values. I've learned a lot about people and discovered most of the executives I work with have six things in common. They all:

1. Care greatly about their families
2. Sacrifice time with their families for the needs of their businesses
3. Are highly compensated for their sacrifices and provide comfortable lifestyles for their families

4. Know that long hours in a high-stress career will affect their health and perhaps reduce the time they have in this world to enjoy their families and the wealth they have created
5. Prefer to remain on this earth longer and have more time with their families and friends
6. Have the financial capability to correct their paths but not the knowledge, tools, or relationships with medical professionals to make changes until it is too late

My parents did not have the financial resources to detect their life-ending ailments ahead of time. They saw our family doctor occasionally, but their care was always reactive and never proactive.

Section 16 officers and corporate insiders are well paid and have the financial resources to course-correct their health. Through the effective management of the compensation programs available to these executives, they not only provide a generous lifestyle for their families today but can implement strategies to improve their health and extend their lifespan and healthspan so they can spend time with their families tomorrow.

This book does not use real names or places, nor does it contain legal or personalized financial advice. *Section 16 Secrets* **is a roadmap to help Section 16 officers (and other corporate insiders) maximize their wealth and their health.**

PART 1

SECTION 16
GPS

CHAPTER 1

SEC REPORTING

"Luck is what happens when preparation meets opportunity."
—SENECA, ROMAN PHILOSOPHER

The first pillar of the *Section 16 GPS* process is *Guidance*. We will cover this pillar through Chapter 8.

Tom and Sarah will reap the rewards of new compensation programs, but the SEC and perhaps some media outlets will now scrutinize their finances. They need guidance on how to move forward.

We will review specific guidance for Tom and Sarah related to these new compensation programs later in the book. First, it is best we review the root of their new Section 16 problems: the SEC.

After the stock market crash of 1929, the SEC was created by Congress to help restore the public's confidence in financial markets. It requires the Section 16 designation for all directors, officers, and 10 percent shareholders of publicly traded companies, specifically the following:

- President
- Principal financial officer
- Principal accounting officer
- Any vice president in charge of a principal business unit, division, or function (such as sales, administration, or finance)
- Any other officer who performs a policy-making function

The SEC's requirement to name all directors, officers, and 10 percent shareholders of publicly traded companies were created to reduce the likelihood of stock manipulation by the small number of speculators who owned concentrated equity positions. This increased transparency of stock ownership was devised to reduce insider trading and other manipulative practices in the public markets.

According to Congress:

> The most potent weapon against the abuse of inside information is full and prompt publicity.

and

> To give investors an idea of the purchases and sales by insiders which may, in turn, indicate their private opinion as to the prospects of the company.

If the public is aware of the purchases and sales an insider makes, it informs the public of the insider's feelings about the company.

For example, an insider might tell the public the outlook for their company has never been brighter, but how would the public feel if the day before an insider makes that comment they sold stock in the company? If the public knows when insiders are buying or selling, it is an indication of their private opinion, regardless of what they say to the public.

The SEC requires Tom and Sarah to provide Silica-Corp an accounting of their holdings in the company's stock. Tom is considered a *beneficial owner* of any shares held by his immediate family members living in his household, so Tom also needs to report shares owned and transacted by his children. This ensures public disclosure of the entire family's activities related to stock ownership.

SEC FORMS

Form 3: Initial Statement of Beneficial Ownership of Securities
Tom and Sarah will use Form 3 to report their initial holdings and their children's holdings within ten days of his promotion.

Form 4: Statement of Changes in Beneficial Ownership
If Tom buys or sells Silica-Corp shares after his initial reporting, he must disclose those transactions and his new share count using Form 4 within two days of the transaction.

Form 5: Annual Statement of Changes in Beneficial Ownership
If Tom's transactions are small, less than $10,000 in a six-month period, those can be reported on Form 5 instead of Form 4. Form 5 is also used if an executive failed to report previous transactions on Form 4. Form 5 is due forty-five days after the company's fiscal year end.

SEC WOES

Thankfully for Tom and Sarah, Silica-Corp has a large corporate legal department. Their legal team ensures the accurate, on-time filing of all the various SEC documents. The company also offers annual training classes to officers to remind them of their reporting requirements.

The sizable legal team at Silica-Corp is a blessing for Tom and Sarah, but others have not been as fortunate. Our client Sam works for a much smaller business, but it is still a publicly traded company, and he is a Section 16 officer. We will call this company SmallCapCorp.

Sam received the initial SEC guidelines from the business's corporate counsel immediately after his promotion, but their counsel did not thoroughly explain the beneficial ownership rules. As a small company, SmallCapCorp did not have Silica-Corp's resources—their legal "department" was just one attorney.

Sam has three college-age children, one of whom is interested in investing his own money. We will call him Sam Jr. or SJ.

SJ is an independent young man studying finance at a prestigious university. He accumulated $10,000 in a savings account from two summers' worth of internships and opened a trading account with an online brokerage firm to start investing independently. He did not want his father's help with his brokerage account, and he was not interested in our firm's input. He wanted to be self-directed.

SJ never discussed his brokerage account with his father, other than to say he purchased a mixture of mutual funds and individual stocks. As you may have guessed, one of the companies he bought stock in was SmallCapCorp.

Neither Sam nor I knew of SJ's position in SmallCapCorp until over a year later. SJ graduated from college and asked if our firm could review his portfolio. When I looked at his online brokerage statement and saw the position in SmallCapCorp, I questioned if SJ had told his father of his investment (the amount was small—only 100 shares worth approximately $2,000), and he said no.

The purchase of SmallCapCorp stock was an honest mistake on SJ's part, and it turned out it was not SJ's fault at all. Sam never told SJ about the beneficial ownership rules, and it is unclear if those rules were ever fully explained *to* Sam by SmallCapCorp's attorney.

BENEFICIAL OWNERSHIP

A Section 16 officer is deemed to beneficially own any security in which they hold a pecuniary interest—the opportunity to share in any profit from a transaction. Insiders are deemed to have a pecuniary interest in securities held by members of their immediate family living in the same household. Family members include all biological and adopted children, stepchildren, parents, stepparents, grandparents, grandchildren, siblings, and in-laws.

Sam now had a problem. His ownership in SmallCapCorp had increased via the beneficial ownership of SJ's shares, but Sam never reported the change to the SEC.

Since SJ's investment was only $2,000, immediate disclosure on Form 4 was not required. Sam could have reported the investment on Form 5 after the end of SmallCapCorp's fiscal year. However, since Sam never knew of the purchase until after a year had passed, Sam had to report it late.

Sam told his corporate counsel what happened, and SmallCap-Corp filed the required forms late. SmallCapCorp also had to disclose in their annual proxy statement that Sam had failed to file the necessary documents on time.

The SEC has the authority to fine Section 16 officers up to $150,000 for filing requirement violations. Thankfully, that did not occur in Sam's case; however, even without any monetary penalties, it was still embarrassing.

Other officers have not been as lucky. In 2014, the SEC announced charges against thirty-four corporate insiders and companies for violating laws requiring the prompt reporting of transactions and holdings. These Section 16 officers were each ordered to pay fines between $25,000 and $100,000 for their late filings. Not only embarrassing but costly.

HOW MANY SECTION 16 OFFICERS ARE THERE?

We have discussed two Section 16 officers, Tom and Sam, but how many Section 16 officers are out there?

There are over 5,000 publicly traded companies in the United States. Publicly traded companies employ approximately one-third of the nonfarm private-sector workforce, so the employee base at these companies is over 43 million employees. Each of these companies typically have between six and twelve Section 16 officers, for a total of 30,000–60,000 corporate insiders (approximately 0.1 percent of the workforce in publicly traded companies).

For our review, we are looking at only *employee* officers. Section 16 also requires reporting from directors and 10 percent shareholders, which we will not cover.

In addition to disclosing stock ownership of Section 16 officers, companies must disclose the total compensation package of their CEO, CFO, and the next three highest-paid employees. Section 16 officers are typically the most highly compensated in the company, with pay packages ranging from the high-six to sometimes nine figures.

Section 16 officers and corporate insiders have onerous reporting requirements, but the financial rewards are substantial. In our next chapter, we will review some of Tom and Sarah's new compensation and benefits programs.

CHAPTER 2

COMPENSATION COMPONENTS FOR SECTION 16 OFFICERS

"My belief is firm in a law of compensation. The true rewards are ever in proportion to the labor and sacrifices made."

—NIKOLA TESLA

Tom and Sarah felt fortunate and were comfortable with his compensation, pre-Section 16 officer. His base salary was $312,000 annually, and he received a bonus each spring that ranged from $25,000 to $100,000. The company also rewarded Tom periodically with employee stock options that vested over time. Tom and Sarah never counted on the bonuses or stock options, so they reinvested any windfall proceeds from those programs.

Tom's new position as a Section 16 officer came with many changes to his compensation package. One change was that

Silica-Corp now linked a large portion of its compensation to company performance and stock performance.

Tom's total compensation is set as a "target," and his target is $1.7 million per year. Tom's division, and the company as a whole, need to meet specific performance metrics for Tom to achieve the full target payment. If performance is poor, his compensation will fall below the target, but if performance exceeds expectations, his income will be higher.

Tom's new base salary is $468,000, or approximately 27 percent of his target compensation of $1.7 million. The other 73 percent of his target compensation comes from the following categories:

- Company and division performance bonuses (18 percent)
- Cash performance awards (27 percent)
- Employee stock options (14 percent)
- Restricted shares and restricted share units (14 percent)

Let us look at how each of these categories supports his "target" compensation.

VARIABLE COMPENSATION: COMPANY AND DIVISION PERFORMANCE BONUSES

Each year, Silica-Corp sets performance targets for the company and each of its business units. If Tom's division and the company hit their performance targets, Tom will receive a bonus equal to 65 percent of his base salary. Half of the bonus is determined by division performance, with the other half linked to how the entire company performed.

This bonus was a significant increase from all previous positions in his career. The largest bonus Tom received in his former job was $100,000—as a Section 16 officer, his bonus could be $304,000 (65 percent of his $468,000 base salary).

Just as Silica-Corp references his overall compensation as a "target," the bonuses are also "targets." The target range for Tom is 0 percent to 250 percent. If his manufacturing division and the company as a whole hit 100 percent of their annual performance target, Tom will receive 100 percent of his bonus—the full $304,000. If the division/company performance is 25 percent of the target, Tom will receive 25 percent of the target bonus, or $76,000. If the division/company performance is 150 percent of the target, Tom will receive 150 percent of the target bonus, or $456,000.

To both Tom and Sarah, the thought of a $456,000 bonus was incredible. There was a downside, though. If the combined division and company performance fell too far below the stated goals, the bonus could be $0.

CASH PERFORMANCE AWARDS

Unlike the bonuses paid out annually, other compensation components are "long-term incentives."

Each year, Tom will receive a cash performance award that will vest in three years. If Tom were to leave the company before the vesting date, he would receive nothing. Like the annual bonuses, this award has a target range. The award is subject to a 0 percent to 250 percent payout range based on three-year performance goals. Silica-Corp pays the cash award after the three-year vesting period (assuming company and division performance is positive).

EMPLOYEE STOCK OPTIONS

Employee stock options are among the most common vehicles companies use to reward their executives. Options will give Tom the right, but not the obligation, to purchase Silica-Corp shares at a predetermined price in the future.

That predetermined purchase price (called the grant price or strike price) is typically equal to the stock price when Silica-Corp grants the options. The options will usually have a lifespan of ten years. Like the cash performance awards, options have a vesting schedule, so they are also considered long-term incentives.

Once the options vest, the employee has the right to purchase shares from the company at that predetermined grant price. If the company's share price increases over time, the difference between the stock price in the future and the original grant price could be substantial. The ability to purchase stock in the future at today's prices provides an excellent employee incentive.

Here is an example:

STOCK OPTION GRANT

Grant: 30,000 options (the right to purchase 30,000 shares)

Grant Price: $50 (the current market price)

Stock Price When Exercised: $90 (the hypothetical price when exercised/sold)

Profit When Exercised: $1,200,000 ($90 minus $50 multiplied by 30,000)

When the employee exercises the option and purchases the stock, they have the right to hold on to those shares in hopes of future appreciation, or they can sell the shares immediately and lock in their profit. Exercising and immediately selling is called a same-day exercise/sale.

The decision to hold the shares received from the exercise or sell them immediately can affect the taxation. Taxation depends on whether the option was a nonqualified stock option (NQSO) or an incentive stock option (ISO).

An NQSO exercise (the purchase of shares) immediately generates ordinary income tax liability. It makes no difference if the newly purchased shares are held or sold.

An ISO (sometimes called a statutory or qualified stock option) offers the potential for more favorable tax treatment. The option exercise itself does not trigger any immediate income tax consequences (but is counted for alternative minimum taxes). The sales date of the newly purchased shares determines the tax treatment. If the future sale meets specific criteria, called a *qualifying disposition*, the ISO profit could qualify for long-term capital gains treatment.

QUALIFYING DISPOSITION

Sales must meet both requirements below:

One-Year Rule: ISO shares are not sold for at least one year after the exercise date.

Two-Year Rule: ISO shares are not sold for at least two years after the options were granted to the employee.

If the sale does not meet both rules for a qualifying disposition, ordinary income taxes will apply on the *bargain element*. The bargain element is the difference between the grant price and the exercise price.

Employees are limited to receiving $100,000 of ISO grants per year. The IRS treats any ISO grants over this amount as NQSO grants.

RESTRICTED SHARES AND RESTRICTED SHARE UNITS

In keeping with the "pay for performance" mindset of Silica-Corp, Tom is also eligible for *restricted shares*.

Restricted shares are shares of Silica-Corp stock, but Tom's ability to trade those shares is *restricted*—Tom cannot transfer or sell those shares until after specific requirements are met, such as corporate performance metrics. There is a risk of forfeiture if Tom leaves Silica-Corp before the shares vest.

Even though Tom cannot transact the shares while they are restricted, he still retains voting authority over those shares, and he is entitled to whatever dividends are paid by the company.

Tom has no immediate tax liability when Silica-Corp grants the restricted stock award. Tom will be taxed when the shares vest, and he is allowed to sell them.

When the shares vest, Tom will pay ordinary income taxes on the difference in value between the vesting date and the grant date. In most cases, the grant's initial value is zero because of the restriction, so 100 percent of the stock's fair market value on the day of release is the taxable profit.

Once the stock is released, the shares are now *unrestricted* and Tom is free to transact the shares just as he could for any other investment.

On the day the stock becomes unrestricted and Tom pays taxes on the fair market value, that fair market value becomes his cost basis. When Tom ultimately sells the shares, he will have a capital gain (or loss), with his tax rate determined by the holding period from the day of release. If Tom holds the shares at least twelve months from the date of release, any gain since that date will qualify for long-term capital gains treatment.

RESTRICTED SHARES OR UNITS

Grant: 10,000 shares or units

Share Price on Vesting Date: $50

Taxable Compensation on Vesting Date: $500,000

Some companies prefer to issue restricted share units (RSUs) instead of restricted shares. An RSU is an unsecured promise by the company to issue shares after the vesting schedule and performance metrics are satisfied. Tom has no voting authority over his RSUs until the share issuance. Once the RSUs vest and shares are issued and delivered, Tom will owe ordinary income tax on the shares' fair market value.

A WORD ABOUT DIVIDENDS

If Tom is issued restricted shares, he is entitled to the shares' dividends. If Tom receives RSUs, there are no dividends since Tom does not own actual shares (just the right to acquire stock from the RSUs in the future).

Some companies decide to pay a "dividend equivalent" to their RSU holders. The dividend equivalent is the same amount as the regular dividend, so RSU holders receive the same benefit as other shareholders.

Silica-Corp can pay dividends and dividend equivalents on a current or deferred basis. If paid on a current basis, Tom will receive the dividend concurrent with other (nonrestricted) shareholders. A deferral of the dividend or equivalent means the payment occurs once the restricted shares or RSUs have vested. These deferred payments result in multiple years of dividends paid in a lump sum on the vesting date.

EXECUTIVE ALLOWANCE BENEFITS

One last compensation component Tom and Sarah are entitled to is reserved for Section 16 officers and other upper-level executives of Silica-Corp.

Tom will receive a $50,000 *executive allowance* each year. An executive allowance plan reimburses executives for expenses related to certain perquisites or "perks."

Common examples of allowable expenses:

- **Professional Fees:** Silica-Corp will reimburse Tom and Sarah for expenses they incur for wealth management planning, investment planning, tax counsel and preparation, estate planning, and attorney fees.
- **Computer and IT Services:** Silica-Corp will reimburse Tom and Sarah for private computer consultants and information technology support for their personal computers and home network.
- **Personal and Home Security:** Silica-Corp will reimburse Tom and Sarah for the cost of any home security services or companies they employ.
- **Corporate Aircraft:** Tom and Sarah can utilize Silica-Corp's company jet for personal use (subject to certain restrictions). The cost of their personal use can be paid for by their executive allowance benefit.

By the conclusion of our meeting, Tom and Sarah had a better understanding of his new $1.7 million target compensation. They also recognized how easy it would be to become overweighted in company stock since so much of Tom's compensation was stock based.

In subsequent meetings, we will discuss different strategies to maximize their new compensation plan and how to protect them from an abundance of company stock.

But first, there was one more benefit they would receive that was *not* available in Tom's previous position. In our next chapter, we will review the unique *pension* benefits for Section 16 officers.

CHAPTER 3

EXCLUSIVE RETIREMENT PLANS

"The question isn't at what age I want to retire; it's at what income."

—GEORGE FOREMAN

In our last chapter, we reviewed Tom's new compensation components. Now we have an opportunity to look at the unique retirement plans reserved for officers of Silica-Corp.

Tom was told that he could defer almost all of his income until retirement if he wanted to, but is that a good idea?

Tom contributes the maximum to his pretax 401(k) plan, currently $20,500, and since he is over age 50, he can make an additional $6,500 "catch-up" contribution, for a total of $27,000 annually (2022 limits).

As a percentage of his base salary of $468,000, a $27,000 401(k) contribution is only a 5.77 percent contribution rate.

The new plans available to Tom are known as Section 409A nonqualified deferred compensation plans. These plans allow for a significantly higher contribution rate.

SUPPLEMENTAL-DEFINED CONTRIBUTION PLAN

Like his 401(k) plan, Tom can defer compensation from his base salary and bonuses into Silica-Corp's 409A supplemental defined contribution plan. Tom can invest his contributions in the same or similar investment options available within his 401(k) plan. Taxes are not due on that deferred compensation in the current year.

Tom will also defer taxes on any investment earnings. No taxes are due until he takes withdrawals in the future, ideally scheduled for after Tom's retirement date, when he may be in a lower tax bracket.

Silica-Corp does not limit how much an employee can contribute to the 409A plan, so Tom can defer 100 percent of his income if he would like. Alternatively, he can choose to defer a more modest amount of his base salary, perhaps 15–25 percent, and then defer 100 percent of his bonus compensation.

A retirement plan with unlimited contributions and unlimited tax deferral until retirement? Deferring 100 percent of your compensation sounds too good to be true.

WHAT'S THE CATCH?

Tom's 401(k) plan is a *qualified* plan and subject to the Employment Retirement Income Security Act (ERISA) of 1974. ERISA is a federal law that sets minimum standards for corporate retirement plans to protect the employees covered by these plans. ERISA mandates the segregation of all employee contributions from the company's assets. Silica-Corp cannot touch the 401(k) dollars if they ever had financial difficulties. Even in the case of bankruptcy by Silica-Corp, Tom's 401(k) dollars are safe.

A 409A plan is *nonqualified*, which means the income Tom defers is not in a segregated account—the deferrals are considered a general asset of Silica-Corp. Some companies only record deferrals as a bookkeeping entry, with no actual cash set aside. For those companies, the deferred income is only a "promise to pay" in the future—a corporate version of an IOU.

If Silica-Corp went bankrupt, Tom's account would be subject to forfeiture, since other creditors might have priority in a liquidation event. Because of this risk, the IRS (and Silica-Corp) allows for unlimited income deferrals to the plan.

Tom must decide to defer income into the 409A plan *before* earning that income. Most companies will require a decision in the fourth quarter prior to the deferral year. Once Tom makes a deferral election, that decision is irrevocable. If something changes in Tom's financial life a few months into the new year, he cannot alter his contribution amount. He needs to wait until the following year.

At the time of Tom's deferral election, he must also decide on a future payment schedule. The payments will usually start at a set point in the future, such as five or ten years from the deferral date, or Tom's retirement date. Tom must also decide if he wishes to receive the payout in the form of a lump sum or a series of annuity payments over time.

PROS

- Tom can defer significant income to help reduce his current tax liability and improve his retirement savings.
- There is no limit to his contributions like in his qualified 401(k) plan.
- Tom can postpone receiving income today when he is in the highest tax bracket, in exchange for receipt in later years when he may be in a lower tax bracket.

CONS

- Tom's deferrals, plus any investment earnings, are subject to forfeiture if Silica-Corp gets into financial difficulty.
- Tom must make his election to defer income into the plan *before* the calendar year he earns that income.
- Once Tom has deferred money into the plan, he cannot access it until the predetermined payout date (usually at retirement). Although early withdrawals from qualified 401(k) plans are discouraged, employees still have access to hardship withdrawals. Hardship withdrawals are not allowed from 409A plans.
- Unlike his 401(k) plan, when Tom retires or otherwise separates from service, he cannot roll over his 409A plan balance into an IRA to extend his tax deferral. Once Tom receives payments from the 409A plan, those payments are immediately taxable as ordinary income.

WHAT SHOULD I DO?

Tom was initially excited about the prospect of saving additional money through Silica-Corp's 409A plan, but he was nervous that he could forfeit his savings should Silica-Corp get into financial trouble.

I explained that Tom should not take the risk of forfeiture lightly. Still, he could rest a little easier knowing that everyone in a decision-making capacity at Silica-Corp also participates in the plan. The management team at Silica-Corp had a big incentive to properly steward the company and protect future payments from the 409A plan.

Tom was comfortable with the financial footing of Silica-Corp, but there have been companies with 409As that have failed in the past. My recommendation was that Tom participate with a deferral of 15–20 percent of his salary and bonus compensation. This deferral will amplify his wealth significantly more than the traditional qualified 401(k) plan alone.

SUPPLEMENTAL EXECUTIVE RETIREMENT PLANS

Silica-Corp has a traditional, defined-benefit pension plan available to all employees. The plan pays out a fixed monthly benefit at retirement based on an employee's income and years of service. That plan is a qualified plan and subject to ERISA protection.

Silica-Corp also has a supplemental executive retirement plan (SERP). The SERP is a unique nonqualified, defined-benefit plan under Section 409A and is a huge wealth amplifier. This plan is available only to select company executives, including *all* Section 16 officers. ERISA laws do not protect the SERP, since it excludes most nonexecutive employees of Silica-Corp. Like the supplemental defined *contribution* plan available to Tom, this defined *benefit* plan is a "promise to pay" by Silica-Corp. If the financials of Silica-Corp should deteriorate, the SERP benefits could be reduced or eliminated.

Tom becomes eligible for the SERP once he reaches ten or more years of service with Silica-Corp. The SERP provides a maximum payment of 50 percent of nonstock-based compensation, calculated by multiplying Tom's years of service by 2 percent. The SERP percentage applies to Tom's highest consecutive sixty months of base salary and bonus compensation. If Tom retires with ten years of service, his annual pension would equal 20 percent of his salary and bonus. With twenty-five years of service, he would reach the maximum 50 percent payout.

Tom has worked for Silica-Corp for twenty-two years and participates in the regular, qualified pension plan—the plan offered to all employees. How much different is the SERP? he asked.

Silica-Corp must offer their qualified pension plan to all employees. Because the qualified plan covers everyone, it has a much smaller payout ratio than the SERP. Silica-Corp's qualified pension plan provides a pension equal to 1.5 percent of an employee's average base salary over their last five years of employment, multiplied by their years of service.

Since qualified pension plans must be offered to all employees, the IRS sets limits to make sure the qualified plans do not unfairly favor highly compensated employees. For 2022, the maximum income that can be considered in qualified plan contributions is $305,000, and the maximum qualified pension payout is $245,000 annually.

Tom's base salary in his Section 16 position is $468,000, but only $305,000 of that salary is "counted" in his qualified pension calculations. If Tom retires in five years, he will have twenty-seven years of service. His qualified pension multiplier would be 40.50 percent (1.5 percent × 27). If the $305,000 maximum salary remains the same, his qualified pension would be equal to 40.50 percent of this $305,000 max, or approximately $123,500 annually.

With the SERP, if we assume Tom achieves his target bonus of 65 percent of base salary, his total income "counted" in the new pension plan would be $772,000 ($468,000 base salary plus $304,000 bonus). With a 50 percent payout benefit, Tom's pension through the SERP would be $386,000 annually, or more than three times what the qualified pension plan would pay.

Tom and Sarah were excited about the new plan. A pension of $386,000 was more than what Tom had earned last year, working fifty to sixty hours a week.

Tom then asked a question I hear a lot. "If my pension will be $386,000 per year, do I need to keep saving for retirement, or could we put that money toward other goals? Perhaps purchase a more expensive home or maybe a vacation home? The need to save for retirement seems to have diminished if we can look forward to a $386,000 pension."

WHAT SHOULD I DO?

Since the SERP is a nonqualified plan, it is a promise to pay from Silica-Corp. Should Silica-Corp run into financial difficulties, the future viability of the SERP could be in danger.

If the SERP is discontinued, Tom will still be eligible for his qualified pension benefit, estimated at approximately $123,500 per year. This pension is a nice figure, but it amounts to just a fraction of his base salary and even a smaller percentage of his new target compensation of $1.7 million.

Since Tom and Sarah can save a large amount of his new compensation, I recommended they assume the SERP will not be there at retirement. If that assumption is wrong and the SERP pays out as planned, they have accumulated additional savings not needed for retirement. Those assets can be used for charitable pursuits or passed on to their children and grandchildren. If the SERP fails or reduces benefits, a successful retirement is still assured by Tom and Sarah who diligently stewarded the resources available to them during their working years.

A CAUTIONARY TALE

The Chrysler Corporation was one of the "big three" US auto manufacturers, and their vehicles were staples on America's roadways for most of the twentieth century. After the financial crisis of 2008, the company filed for bankruptcy protection.

The bankruptcy court's debt restructuring left unsecured creditors with nothing, including more than 400 current and former executives who participated in their nonqualified deferred compensation and supplemental executive retirement plans. Even

Lee Iacocca, the former chairman credited with saving Chrysler in the 1980s, saw his nonqualified pension money disappear.

Chrysler emerged from bankruptcy as a leaner company with much less debt and continues to manufacture cars in the twenty-first century. I am sure those former executives are still upset, because plenty of new Chrysler, Dodge, and Jeep vehicles continue to be seen on the road.

This story is a good reminder of why executives need to make sure they have diversified a portion of their risk away from their employer. I hope those Chrysler executives regularly exercised and sold their employee options and restricted shares and built a portfolio to sustain them in retirement *independent* of their employer's fortunes (or misfortunes).

The exclusive retirement plans available to Section 16 officers are incredibly generous, but they should be considered a supplement to, and not a replacement of, traditional savings and wealth accumulation.

One of the themes I discuss with executives is how to diversify their personal financial future away from their company's. Helping to ensure they do not get overweighted in nonqualified plans is one way to work toward that goal.

The best way to achieve financial independence from your company is through the regular sale of company stock, which we will review in our next chapter.

CHAPTER 4

TRADING WINDOWS, OPTION AND RESTRICTED STOCK STRATEGIES

"People who succeed in the stock market also accept periodic losses, setbacks, and unexpected occurrences. Calamitous drops do not scare them out of the game."

—PETER LYNCH

Tom emailed me in a bit of a panic. Silica-Corp stock declined by 10 percent this week, but the value of his employee options dropped by 35 percent.

Tom would have liked to exercise and sell some of his employee options, but trading was prohibited. Silica-Corp was currently in a restricted or "blackout" period, and trading by Section 16 officers was not allowed.

TRADING WINDOWS AND PRECLEARANCE

The Securities and Exchange Act of 1934 prohibits the purchase or sale of securities based on material nonpublic information (MNPI). Most companies establish four trading windows each year (commencing after their quarterly earnings are announced) to give executives a "window of opportunity" to trade in company shares. The trading windows can be as short as a few days or extended for several weeks. Any dates outside of these windows are called blackout periods, and trading is not allowed. Companies presume the public is aware of all material information during these trading windows.

For Section 16 officers, the rules are slightly different. Even when inside an approved trading window, they still need to seek permission from their company's legal department before transacting shares. This is known as preclearance.

Tom told me he feels stupid he didn't sell his shares earlier. If a 10 percent drop in Silica-Corp stock price can reduce the value of his employee options by 35 percent, what will happen if the stock dropped by 20 or 30 percent? Will his stock options be reduced by 50 percent? What should he do?

This chapter will review the leveraged nature of employee options and strategies for managing both options and restricted shares.

LEVERAGE

The 35 percent drop in the value of Tom's employee options was due to the stock options' leveraged nature. Any move in Silica-

Corp's stock price will result in a more significant adjustment to the value of his employee options.

Let us look at a hypothetical Silica-Corp option grant.

HYPOTHETICAL OPTION GRANT

Option Grant: 10,000 shares

Option Grant Price: $25

Current Share Price: $35

Current Profit: $100,000 ($35 market price minus the $25 grant price, multiplied by 10,000 shares)

If Silica-Corp's stock price goes up by 10 percent, from $35 to $38.50, the option profit will increase to $135,000 ($38.50 market price minus $25 grant price, multiplied by 10,000 shares). *A 10 percent increase* in share price results in a *35 percent increase* in option profit.

If Silica-Corp stock drops by 10 percent, from $35 to $31.50, the option profit will fall to $65,000 ($31.50 market price minus $25 grant price, multiplied by 10,000 shares). *A 10 percent decline* in share price results in a *35 percent decline* in the option profit.

In this example, every $1-per-share increase in Silica-Corp stock price moves the profit of this option higher by $10,000 ($1 per share on 10,000 shares). A $2-per-share increase moves the profit higher by $20,000. A $2-per-share increase on a $35 stock would be approximately 5.7 percent, yet the profit jumps by 20 percent. Likewise, if the stock declined by $2 per share or 5.7 percent, the option profit would fall by 20 percent.

At the beginning of this chapter, Tom's question was, "What if the stock price falls by 20–30 percent? Would I be down 50 percent?"

With this option example above, the answer is much worse. A 25 percent decline in Silica-Corp stock, from $35 to $26.25 per share, results in an *87.5 percent* decline in option profit. The option profit falls from $100,000 to $12,500.

The leveraged nature of employee options allows for accelerated wealth creation when the stock price increases but equally accelerated wealth *destruction* when the price drops.

UNDERSTANDING THE LEVERAGE OF YOUR OPTIONS

We recommend that executives review the amount of leverage for each of their option grants, as it will change based on the grant price and the current market price.

For example:

Grant #	Options Granted	Grant Price	Current Price	Current Option Value	Leverage
1	10,000	$15	$35	$200,000	1.75x
2	10,000	$20	$35	$150,000	2.33x
3	10,000	$25	$35	$100,000	3.5x
4	10,000	$30	$35	$50,000	7x

When we look at the previous chart, we see how leverage correlates to the difference between the grant price and the current market price. The smaller the difference is between those two prices, the greater the leverage.

Grant #1 has a low grant price of $15 per share compared to the current market value of $35 per share. This grant is "in the money" by $20 per share ($35–$15). When the $20 gain is multiplied by the 10,000 share grant, the current profit is $200,000.

To understand the leveraged nature of the stock option grants, let us first examine nonleveraged ownership of Silica-Corp stock. If Tom had $200,000 invested in Silica-Corp stock outright, not part of an option grant, and the share price of Silica-Corp stock increased by 10 percent, Tom's $200,000 investment would increase 10 percent to $220,000.

NONLEVERAGED INVESTMENT

Current Value: $200,000

Investment Gain: +10 percent

Future Value: $220,000

Now let us look at option #1. A 10 percent move in the value of Silica-Corp will move the share price from $35 to $38.50 per share, resulting in a future value of $235,000:

GRANT #1 (WITH 1.75X LEVERAGE)

Current Value: $200,000

Investment Gain: +10 percent ($3.50 per share)

Future Value: $235,000 ($38.50 stock price minus $15 grant price, multiplied by 10,000 shares)

A 10 percent move in a nonleveraged investment resulted in a future value of $220,000, but the same 10 percent move in Grant #1 resulted in a future value of $235,000.

Every 1 percent move from the current share price will move a nonleveraged investment by the same 1 percent.

With Grant #1, every 1 percent move in share price will move the value of the options by 1.75 percent. This leverage is why the future value of Grant #1 moved by $35,000 and not $20,000. What would have usually been a $20,000 gain was amplified by the 1.75x leverage of the option grant.

Now let us look at a nonleveraged investment of $50,000:

NONLEVERAGED INVESTMENT

Current Value: $50,000

Investment Gain: +10 percent

Future Value: $55,000

Let us apply this 10 percent gain to Grant #4:

GRANT #4 (WITH 7X LEVERAGE)

Current Value: $50,000

Investment Gain: +10 percent ($3.50 per share)

Future Value: $85,000 ($38.50 stock price minus $30 grant price, multiplied by 10,000 shares)

At $35 per share, Grant #4 has $5 per share of profit based on the $30 per share grant price. When this $5 per share is multiplied by the 10,000 share grant, the gain is $50,000.

If a nonleveraged investment increases by 10 percent, a $50,000 investment would increase to $55,000. The same 10 percent increase in stock price would move the profit of option Grant #4 higher by $35,000. For every 1 percent move up or down from $35 per share, the option grant will move 7x that amount. A 10 percent move in stock price changes the option profit by 70 percent.

In these previous examples, we assumed a 10 percent move in Silica-Corp stock price, from $35 to $38.50. What would happen if the share price increased by 20 percent, from $35 up to $42?

The same leverage would apply as follows:

Grant #	Options Granted	Grant Price	Current Price	Current Option Value	Share Price Move	New Share Price	New Value	Leverage	Option Return
1	10,000	$15	$35	$200,000	+20%	$42	$270,000	1.75x	+35%
2	10,000	$20	$35	$150,000	+20%	$42	$220,000	2.33x	+47%
3	10,000	$25	$35	$100,000	+20%	$42	$170,000	3.5x	+70%
4	10,000	$30	$35	$50,000	+20%	$42	$120,000	7x	+140%

If Silica-Corp stock moves higher by 20 percent to $42 per share, the value of Grant #1 will move higher by 35 percent (1.75x leverage). The same 20 percent increase would move Grant #4 higher by 140 percent (7x leverage).

WHAT'S THE CATCH?

Leverage looks great when stock prices are increasing. No discussion of leverage would be complete without a deep dive into the downsides to leverage.

Let us look at the same options assuming a 20 percent decline in Silica-Corp stock, from $35 down to $28.

Grant #	Options Granted	Grant Price	Current Price	Current Option Value	Share Price Move	New Share Price	New Value	Leverage	Option Return
1	10,000	$15	$35	$200,000	-20%	$28	$130,000	1.75x	-35%
2	10,000	$20	$35	$150,000	-20%	$28	$80,000	2.33x	-47%
3	10,000	$25	$35	$100,000	-20%	$28	$30,000	3.5x	-70%
4	10,000	$30	$35	$50,000	-20%	$28	$0	7x	-100%

If a regular nonleveraged investment of $200,000 fell by 20 percent, the ending value should be $160,000, for a loss of $40,000. Grant #1 suffers a 35 percent loss from a 20 percent decline in the share price, with an ending value of $130,000. This $70,000 loss is due to the 1.75x leverage.

The greater the leverage, the greater the danger. A 20 percent decline of a nonleveraged investment should bring a $50,000 starting value down to $40,000—a loss of $10,000. Option #4 has done much worse than that. If Silica-Corp stock declines from $35 to $28, option #4 is now "under water." The market price is below the grant price. At this point, the value of option #4 is zero. Even though the stock price declined by only 20 percent, the higher leverage in option #4 results in a 100 percent loss.

HOW DO WE USE LEVERAGE TO OUR ADVANTAGE?

Something not illustrated in the previous examples was the options' expiration date. Let us suppose the options each have a ten-year lifespan and were granted at different points in time as follows:

Grant #	Options Granted	Current Option Value	Grant Date	Expiration Date	Leverage
1	10,000	$200,000	Jan. 2014	Jan. 2024	1.75x
2	10,000	$150,000	Jan. 2015	Jan. 2025	2.33x
3	10,000	$100,000	Jan. 2016	Jan. 2026	3.5x
4	10,000	$50,000	Jan. 2017	Jan. 2027	7x

If all things were equal, we would typically recommend exercising the options with the closest expiration date first, since the stock would have less time to recover from adverse movement.

What if all things were not equal? What if a competitor of Silica-Corp recently announced poor earnings and investors are nervous about the entire sector? What if the overall economy showed signs of slowing, potentially impacting the broader stock market?

In situations where there is a negative outlook for the company, industry, or overall economy/stock market, the most leveraged options pose the greatest risk to the option portfolio.

If Tom and Sarah planned to raise cash from an option exercise and the company's outlook was poor, removing Grant #4 from the portfolio would eliminate the most leverage and therefore the most downside risk. Even though this option has a long life left before expiration, a 20 percent stock price decline results in a 100 percent loss of the option's current profit (due to the leverage).

Suppose the grant had another eight to nine years to go before expiration. In that case, an aggressive investor might feel confident they could recover from any downturn in the stock over an extended holding period. With more than half of the life of Grant #4 already behind us, the risk of the stock declining and not recovering in time is much greater.

Now let us suppose the outlook for the company is more bullish. In this example, the leverage of Grant #4 works in Tom's favor. An increase of 20 percent in the value of Silica-Corp from current levels would result in a 140 percent increase of the current option profit.

Tom and Sarah may want to hold Grant #4 longer, so they

should consider exercising Grant #1 to generate their cash target (the grant with the least leverage). If Silica-Corp stock were to jump 20 percent higher before expiration, they have given up a potential gain of $35,000 in option Grant #1 (the grant with 1.75x leverage) in favor of the $70,000 increase achieved in Grant #4 (with 7x leverage).

TOO CLOSE

All this makes sense "on paper," but it is challenging to predict future values accurately in the real world. Corporate executives are sometimes "too close" to the company to have an objective outlook. They spend their days motivating their employees, and many also have daily or weekly interactions with investors and institutions, so their message usually needs to be positive. All of this tends to make their outlook a bit rosier than an unaffiliated analyst.

Most publicly traded companies have a handful of analysts and research firms following their stock, and many executives in the C-suite tend to have a love-hate relationship with them. Still, I recommend looking at the consensus analyst opinion, because that is what other investors are doing.

I suggested to Tom and Sarah that we put together a list of target prices to consider exercising some of their options. We could then match an appropriate option grant to those target prices based on the analyst outlook. Tom expects Silica-Corp to open a trading window for Section 16 officers within the next month. He wants to be prepared to exercise options if Silica-Corp's share price hits any of our predetermined price targets.

RESTRICTED SHARES

Unlike the employee options that utilize leverage, restricted shares or RSUs have no leverage.

Let us look at some hypothetical restricted shares:

Year	Shares Granted	Share Price	Current Value	Release Date
2019	4,000	$35	$140,000	March 2022
2020	5,000	$35	$175,000	March 2023
2021	6,000	$35	$210,000	March 2024

Each of these grants has a different value, but that is due to the number of shares granted, because there is no leverage. A 1 percent move in Silica-Corp stock will move the restricted shares by the same percentage.

Unlike the options that provide Tom with some leeway to determine when to exercise and generate taxable income, the restricted shares' release schedule is predetermined. Tom cannot change or alter that timeline.

With no leverage to examine and no timing required, are there any trading strategies for the restricted shares?

In almost all cases, if the executive is in an open trading window, the most appropriate strategy for restricted shares is to sell them as soon as they are released. Otherwise, do it as soon as the next trading window opens.

Whenever an executive has a "sell" decision to make, it is human nature to wonder, *Is this a good price?* Because of that, it is my opinion that many holders of restricted shares or RSUs make a mistake upon vesting—they hold on to their newly vested shares, instead of selling them immediately, for one of two reasons:

1. They want to hold on to the shares because they want the future gain to qualify for long-term capital gains treatment.

or

2. They want to hold on to the shares because they believe the stock is undervalued.

With restricted shares or RSUs, the executive is taxed at ordinary income tax rates based on the fair market value of the shares on the release date. It makes no difference if the executive sells or holds the shares. Retaining newly released shares for twelve months past the release date only qualifies any future gain for long-term capital gains treatment. Why take the risk of an additional twelve-month holding period when any tax benefit will only apply to future profits?

Another common mistake is believing the stock is undervalued and using that belief as a reason to hold the shares. Perhaps the stock is undervalued, but since the taxable income is equal to the release date value, I would prefer to see the executive sell the shares for an amount close to what they were taxed on. Even though holding on to the shares could result in additional gains if the share price increases, the opposite is true if the share price falls.

I remember a situation from 2001 when an executive received shares worth approximately $250,000 on the release date and did not want to sell them. The dot-com bubble had burst, and most stock prices were down. His company withheld 20 percent of the newly released shares for taxes, and the executive retained the remaining shares.

When he prepared his 2001 income tax return in the spring of 2002, he learned that his federal tax rate was approximately 40 percent, not the 20 percent withheld at the time of release.

The executive needed to sell $50,000 worth of stock to cover his tax bill, but by the spring of 2002, the stock price was *half* as much as it was on the initial release date.

When I ask executives that question, most of them state they would not purchase shares on the open market. When I ask why, the answer is almost always, "Because I have too much company stock already."

Sometimes it can be difficult to understand that the decision to "not sell" newly released shares is no different from purchasing new shares.

STOCK OWNERSHIP GUIDELINES

There is one exception to the sale recommendation for newly released shares. Most companies require their Section 16 officers maintain a certain amount of company stock in their portfolio. This ownership requirement shows both existing and potential investors that the officer has aligned their interests with shareholders. If an officer has not yet met their share ownership requirement, it may be necessary to maintain the restricted shares after release.

At Silica-Corp, Tom must own shares worth 3x his base salary of $468,000, for a total of $1.4 million.

For new Section 16 officers, companies may allow executives to meet the ownership requirement over time. For Tom, Silica-Corp requires him to meet the ownership target within five years. Until he meets the ownership requirement, Tom is prohibited from selling any restricted shares, even once released.

In our next chapter, we will review how Tom and Sarah can work around the trading windows and blackout periods required by Silica-Corp to give them more opportunities to reduce their exposure to Silica-Corp stock.

CHAPTER 5

TRADING PLANS, SHORT-SWING PROFIT RULES, AND SPECIAL ELECTION STRATEGIES

"Speculation is an effort, probably unsuccessful, to turn a little money into a lot. Investment is an effort, which should be successful, to prevent a lot of money from becoming a little."

—FRED SCHWED JR.

Tom understands the need to exercise options regularly and sell his restricted shares as quickly as possible, but his opportunities to do so are limited.

As we reviewed in our last chapter, Section 16 officers are limited to just a few trading windows each year.

Tom's new position will expose him to material nonpublic information (MNPI), which can impair his ability to sell shares even inside the trading windows. I told him we could accommodate a systematic sale of his securities via a specialized trading plan.

10B5-1 TRADING PLANS

The SEC adopted rule 10b5-1 in 2000. Included in this rule is executives' ability to establish a written trading plan to be executed in the future. If the executive schedules transactions via a preplanned written trading plan, the executive is deemed to have an "affirmative defense" against allegations of trading while in possession of MNPI.

An affirmative defense does not protect the executive from allegations of misconduct, but a properly executed trading plan should allow the executive to prevail during any inquiries.

FIVE STEPS TO ESTABLISH A 10B5-1 TRADING PLAN

Properly executing a 10b5-1 trading plan is relatively easy—just five steps:

1. The plan should specify the number of shares to be sold, the share price, and the transaction date, or a written formula or trigger points to determine those details.
2. The executive must implement the plan during a time when the executive does not possess any MNPI. For most executives, the best time to establish the trading plan would be shortly after the company's quarterly earnings are announced, during an open trading window.
3. The plan should have a waiting period, perhaps thirty to ninety days, before any trades could occur. This waiting

period will further reduce the appearance that the executive implemented the trading plan to trade on MNPI.

4. The executive should have only one trading plan in force at a time. Multiple trading plans could suggest the executive intended to hedge or otherwise alter the trades triggered under a previous plan, which would weaken the affirmative defense argument.

5. Although the SEC does not impose time limits on the terms of a trading plan, they are a recommended best practice. Any time limit must avoid the appearance of impropriety. For example, implementing a new trading plan each quarter would weaken the affirmative defense claim.

AFFIRMATIVE DEFENSE CLAIMS

What are affirmative defense claims, and what do they have to do with trading plans?

An affirmative defense claim is meant to excuse the defendant from civil and criminal liability. The SEC allows an affirmative defense claim if an executive trades in securities via a trading plan, even if the executive is aware of MNPI on the day of execution. This holds true as long as the trading plan that triggered the trades was adopted before the executive became aware of the MNPI and provides written instructions to determine the amount, price, and date of the trades. It also must prohibit the executive from exercising any subsequent influence over the trades and that the trades (purchases or sales) are made in compliance with the trading plan.

Finally, the trading plan must be entered into in "good faith" and not part of a plot or scheme to circumvent the rules against trading, based on MNPI. Trading plans aid in affirmative defense claims.

TRADING PLAN BENEFITS FOR THE EXECUTIVE

Trading plans provide more than just an affirmative defense claim. With a trading plan, executives can establish systematic trigger points for reducing exposure to company stock and do not need to seek preclearance for every trade—they only need permission to establish the trading plan.

They can potentially have trades triggered and executed multiple times per year, independent of the predetermined trading windows. Trading plans may provide executives more opportunities to diversify away from company stock. Trading plans also remove short-term emotion from trading decisions for executives, since the trading plan is implemented well in advance of any trade execution.

Trading plans can provide executives with an affirmative defense against insider trading accusations and reduce the need for them to explain trades to the press, investors, stock analysts, or fellow employees. The question is no longer, "Did the executive know of any MNPI at the time of the trade?" but rather, "Did the executive know of any MNPI at the adoption of the trading plan?"

TRADING PLAN BENEFITS FOR THE COMPANY

Trading plans are beneficial to all parties, including the company. The trading plan provides the company with an affirmative defense to insider trading allegations for executives who made trades according to the plan. If the executive established triggers for trades months ahead of the actual sales, the company might face less scrutiny and negative publicity from insider selling.

The trading plan and affirmative defense will decrease the company's compliance burden. Normally, the company must determine if an executive has any MNPI each time the executive wants to buy or sell company stock. With a trading plan, however, the company only has to determine compliance when the executive implemented it.

EXAMPLES OF TRADING PLAN USES

An executive...

1. Required to make quarterly estimated tax payments might adopt a trading plan to sell shares each quarter ahead of the tax bill due date.

2. With children in college might adopt a trading plan to sell shares every July and December ahead of tuition payments coming due.

3. Might want to purchase a beach home in the next eighteen months. They could set specific price targets to exercise employee options over that predetermined period.

4. Who has not yet met the stock ownership guidelines for their position, might set a goal to purchase a specific dollar amount of shares on the first Monday of each quarter, over the next year.

SHORT-SWING PROFIT RULES

A short-swing profit occurs when a transaction generates gains within a six-month window.

If a Section 16 officer buys and later sells company shares inside six months, any profits must be surrendered and returned to the company. The same rule applies if the officer sells stock first and later buys shares within six months.

The highest sales price is matched against the lowest purchase price in the six-month window to determine the short-swing profits. This calculation could result in "deemed profits," even if the executive lost money on the individual transactions.

It is also important to remember the issues caused by beneficial ownership. If the insider sells stock at $35 per share, but two months later, a family member purchases stock at $25 per share, a short-swing profit has occurred.

Section 16 imposes a strict liability standard on all insiders. The company cannot waive its right to recover the short-swing profits if they exist. Honest mistakes made in good faith, or a misunderstanding of the law, are not acceptable defenses.

SECTION 83(B) ELECTION

There is no immediate taxation on newly granted restricted shares, due to the risk of forfeiture before vesting. Once vested and released, ordinary income tax rates apply to the market value of the shares.

The fair market value of the shares on the release date becomes the cost basis for those shares. Capital gains taxes will apply to any subsequent sale of the shares, based on the holding period, since the release date. If the executive sells shares within one year of the release date, the gain or loss is taxed at short-term capital gains rates. If the shares are sold more than a year after release, they qualify for long-term capital gains rates.

To protect the executive from paying taxes on shares that risk forfeiture, the IRS does not tax the restricted shares until they are vested and released. Suppose the executive would like to waive that protection by voluntarily paying taxes when the restricted shares are issued. In exchange for paying taxes up front, the executive can receive capital gains treatment on 100 percent of the future profit of the grant. This voluntary tax payment is known as an 83(b) election.

The IRS allows the executive to submit an 83(b) election within thirty days of being granted the restricted shares. An 83(b) election notifies the IRS that the executive has voluntarily decided to pay taxes on the restricted shares on the grant date, even though there is a risk of forfeiture before vesting.

By paying taxes immediately, the cost basis equals the value on the grant's issue date and not the future release date. If the stock is ultimately sold more than a year after the issue date, all profit above the cost basis qualifies for long-term capital gains rates.

For executives like Tom, who are in the highest tax bracket, the difference between ordinary income tax rates and long-term capital gains rates can be a significant wealth amplifier.

IS IT RIGHT FOR ME?

A Section 83(b) election makes the most sense when the fair market value of the restricted shares is low at the time of the grant. A low valuation will occur most often with startup or early-stage companies. An executive at a young company might be granted 10,000 shares at a nominal value of $1 per share. Paying taxes in advance on an award worth $10,000 is an easy decision if the belief is that those shares will be worth 5x, 10x, or 100x once released. The risk with a new company is that the enterprise might not be successful, and the executive has paid taxes on a grant that could be worthless in the future.

There is less risk of the shares being worthless with mature companies, but with less risk typically comes higher share prices and higher valuation at the time of the grant. A higher initial valuation will require more up-front taxation, if the executive makes a Section 83(b) election. With few exceptions, we typically do not recommend prepaying taxes on grants worth more than $100,000.

In this chapter, we reviewed ways for executives to establish trading plans in compliance with SEC regulations and the importance of the short-swing profit rules, and we looked at ways to reduce future taxation through Section 83(b) elections.

The trading discussion, however, does not end here.

In our next chapter, Tom and Sarah will find out that sometimes Section 16 officers and their families face additional obstacles related to selling company stock—ones that impact them on a personal level.

CHAPTER 6

DO NOT LET THE GROCERY STORE SCARE YOU OUT OF DIVERSIFICATION

"Bulls make money, bears make money, but pigs get slaughtered."

—OLD WALL STREET TRUISM

Fast forward a few years, and Tom has more than satisfied Silica-Corp's stock ownership guidelines. Tom is required to own shares worth 3x his base salary, for a total of $1.4 million worth of company stock.

A few weeks ago, his employee options and shares were worth approximately $3.5 million. Today, that value jumped to $4.75 million, seemingly overnight. The overall stock market moved higher, and Silica-Corp jumped with it. Due to the leverage of the stock options, Tom's holdings increased by 35 percent, and it occurred inside of an approved trading window.

Since Tom owns more shares than the executive ownership guidelines call for, we recommended that he reduce his holdings by approximately 15 percent, and he agreed. Tom received preclearance for the trade from Silica-Corp's legal department to sell $750,000 worth of shares. He executed the transaction and followed all the reporting rules.

The following week, Sarah was in the grocery store, and a friend mentioned Tom's sale. The friend wanted to know if everything was okay with Tom because he sold so much stock. This friend had no connection to Silica-Corp.

How did she know?

The local newspaper wrote a story about insider stock sales in his small town. Tom reported his sale to the SEC, but he did not think it would make the front page of his local newspaper. Would friends or neighbors, who also might be shareholders, believe he was no longer loyal to the company or that he was concerned about the prospects of Silica-Corp? Would it send the wrong message to his direct reports? Would parents of their children's friends mention the stock sale to their kids? Would his children get teased for having a "rich dad"?

The article's focus was not on Tom alone, as three other executives had recently sold stock as well. Still, both Tom and Sarah were shocked to learn that what they thought was a private financial transaction was now quite literally front-page news in their community.

The article disclosed the number of shares Tom sold, the dollar amount of the transaction, and how many shares he continued to hold in Silica-Corp stock. Both Tom and Sarah were embarrassed to see their name next to a $750,000 transaction. "That is more than most homes in our community are worth," they said.

They were also uncomfortable that everyone knew their remaining shares were worth approximately $4 million. How would this affect their relationship with their friends, family, and neighbors? Would they start to receive more solicitations for charitable donations? Would contractors jack up the price for work needed on their home in the future?

The anxiety caused by the newspaper article made Tom and Sarah hesitant to sell stock again—no matter the price. They were private people, and they preferred to stay that way. Perhaps they would hold on to all their shares until retirement and not sell until the Section 16 reporting requirements went away.

DIVERSIFICATION

I told Tom and Sarah to "not let the grocery store scare you out of **diversification**." I reminded them that all their Silica-Corp shares were worth about $3.5 million just a few weeks ago. The stock had a nice jump up, and their shares grew to $4.75 million when we recommended selling $750,000 worth of shares.

In percentage terms, we reduced their company stake by just over 15 percent, and with $4 million of Silica-Corp shares remaining, they still had more company exposure today than they did a few weeks earlier. Another way to look at it is that their stock value had increased by $1.25 million over the past few weeks, and we sold only 60 percent of that increase.

I asked Tom and Sarah how they would feel if the value of their holdings went back down to $3.5 million and they had not sold shares? Tom's name would have stayed out of the newspaper, but they would have missed out on an opportunity to reduce their reliance on company stock for the benefit of their financial future.

I reminded them that the health of Silica-Corp affects their entire financial life, not just the value of their portfolio. Tom's job is directly affected by the health of Silica-Corp, and a large amount of his income comes in the form of stock-based compensation. The value of their home is also tied to the company's health, because if the company fails and unemployment increases in their town, real estate prices may fall. I told them that they do not want to be in a position where they have levered all aspects of their financial life (job, investment portfolio, real estate) to Silica-Corp. To do that, they need to diversify away from Silica-Corp.

Before the recent Silica-Corp move, their net worth (excluding their home) totaled approximately $6 million. Silica-Corp made up 58 percent of this total. After the stock price increase, their net worth moved to $7.25 million, but Silica-Corp now made up 66 percent of the total.

Although Tom was not an officer of the company during the financial crisis of 2008, I reminded him of the hit Silica-Corp took at that time. Most large-company stock mutual funds were down 40 percent in 2008. Silica-Corp was down 60 percent.

Tom did the math and said he would be devastated if his remaining $4 million of options and shares fell by 60 percent. That would take his value from $4 million down to $1.6 million. I told him that the math was worse than that due to the leveraged nature of his employee options. A 60 percent decline in Silica-Corp's share price would reduce his Silica-Corp portfolio by over $3.5 million, for a drop of over 87 percent. This is because the market price of Silica-Corp would be below the initial grant price of some of the options, making some options worthless. When this occurs, those options are considered "under water." If we experienced a repeat of 2008, Tom's $4 million of options and shares would be worth approximately $500,000. Tom's face went white.

Tom and Sarah take on two types of risk with their Silica-Corp portfolio:

1. They have the risk of owning a concentrated equity position.
2. That risk is then magnified by the leverage of their employee options.

Because of this, I told them not to be discouraged by the "public relations" issues of periodically selling shares. As embarrassing as it might be to have their name in the newspaper when they sell shares, they would be more embarrassed if they could not comfortably retire because they missed opportunities to diversify away from Silica-Corp. Their sale of $750,000 of Silica-Corp shares reduced their company stock concentration from 66 percent of their net worth down to about 55 percent. This concentration is still too high, but it is progress

PRIVACY STRATEGY

Sarah asked if there was anything they could do to make the transactions a bit more private.

One way to reduce the likelihood of getting your name in your local newspaper is to try to time your sale *after* the sale of more senior officers in the company. For example, suppose the CEO sells shares at the beginning of the trading window. Once you see the SEC Form 4 filed for that transaction, wait a week or two before making your sale. The CEO's sale would most likely drive any article in the newspaper, and it might also mention other executives who transacted shares around the same date. If you delay your sale a week or two, the newspaper might not run two stories on the same topic within a short period.

Even if you successfully keep your name out of the newspaper, you must still report your transactions on SEC Form 4. Nosy neighbors can find out this information via a quick Google search, but hopefully they are less likely to mention it at the grocery store.

Tom and Sarah now understand that any short-term embarrassment caused by the public nature of their transactions is worth the long-term benefits of reducing their reliance on company stock. In our next chapter, we will review how Tom and Sarah can hedge away the risk of their concentrated equity position in Silica-Corp prior to selling shares.

CHAPTER 7

HEDGING CONCENTRATED EQUITY POSITIONS

"I'm always thinking about losing money as opposed to making money. Don't focus on making money. Focus on protecting what you have."

—PAUL TUDOR JONES

Tom and Sarah took our advice over the years, selling restricted shares periodically and exercising employee options on a regular schedule. Despite those efforts, Tom has still accumulated a large amount of Silica-Corp stock. Tom believes in his company's long-term prospects, but he recognizes that his net worth will suffer if he is wrong. We decided to discuss ways to hedge some of the risks of his concentrated position in Silica-Corp.

Many companies prohibit hedging for their Section 16 officers, but not all companies, and not every executive reading this book is subject to the stringent requirements of Section 16. Those readers will benefit from this review.

COVERED CALL OPTIONS

Tom and Sarah can generate additional cash from their Silica-Corp shares by committing to sell their shares to another investor at a predetermined price in the future. This commitment is known as a *covered call option*. The investor buying the right to purchase their shares would pay Tom and Sarah an up-front payment, known as option premium, to purchase the call option from them.

For example, Tom might receive $0.50 per share by committing to sell 10,000 shares of Silica-Corp (currently at $35 per share) at a $38 per share "future price," sometime over the next three months. At $0.50 per share, that option would pay Tom $5,000.

The investor who owns the call option can require Tom to sell his shares at $38 anytime between now and the option's expiration in three months. If Silica-Corp moves higher to $40, the owner of the call option will "call away" Tom's stock at $38 and then turn around and sell the shares at $40 for a $2 per share profit. In this example, Tom has received the $38 committed sales price, plus the $0.50 per share of up-front cash from the option premium.

If the price of Silica-Corp never moves above $38, the owner of the call option will let the option expire unexercised. The option owner will not pay Tom $38 if the stock is trading in the open market at $35.

Regardless if Tom's shares are sold (called away), Tom keeps the $0.50 per share of premium he received when he sold the option. The investor who purchases the call option from Tom is making a bullish bet on Silica-Corp because the stock price needs to move higher for the owner of the call option to earn a return on the premium they paid. Tom can participate in some upside in Silica-Corp, from $35 up to $38, but he has sold away upside above $38 in exchange for the $0.50 of up-front cash received from the option premium.

For executives like Tom, if covered call options are allowed by their companies, they can provide an income stream *in addition to* whatever dividends the stock might pay. The premium of $0.50 per share is equal to 1.43 percent of the current $35 value of Silica-Corp stock. Earned over three months, 1.43 percent is equivalent to almost 6 percent on an annualized basis.

Covered call options also provide a small amount of downside protection, up to the call option premium received. If Silica-Corp were to fall over three months, it could fall to $34.50 per share without materially affecting Tom because he received $0.50 per share in call option premium. If Silica-Corp stock fell by $1, Tom would participate in only half of that decline because of the $0.50 he already received.

Although covered call options can provide some level of down-side protection, their primary function is to:

1. Allow investors to generate additional income from their shares.
2. Establish predetermined price points at which to sell shares.

Executives who wish to limit their downside by more than what a call option can provide should consider protective put options.

PROTECTIVE PUT OPTIONS

Many companies have put in place anti-hedging policies for their Section 16 officers, banning transactions that might allow an executive to profit from a decline in their company's stock price. If your company allows these transactions, one of the best ways to hedge the downside risk of concentrated equity positions is to utilize publicly traded put options.

A *protective put option* gives the option owner the right to sell stock in the future at a predetermined price. That future price is typically lower than the current stock price, protecting shares from further decline below that price. You can think of a protective put option as an insurance policy.

In our previous covered call option example, Tom and Sarah received option premium (cash) in exchange for their promise to sell someone else their shares in the future. With a protective put option, Tom and Sarah would pay a premium to someone else to act as their insurance policy by setting a minimum sales price for their stock in the future.

For example, if Silica-Corp is trading at $35 per share, you could decide to purchase a put option at a level of $32 per share. This put option would give you the ability to sell shares at $32 over a predetermined time in the future. With this put option, you would take on the first $3 per share of risk (Silica-Corp falling from $35 to $32). Using the "insurance policy" analogy, this $3 per share of risk would be your "deductible."

If Silica-Corp stock fell below $32, you could sell your shares at $32. If Silica-Corp fell to $15, you still have a buyer at $32 via the put option.

Let us suppose the put option's cost was $0.50 per share to protect Silica-Corp against a decline below $32 for the next three months. If an executive wants to protect 10,000 shares, the cost would be $5,000.

If Silica-Corp moves higher to $40 per share, the executive who owns the put option will let it expire unexercised. Why sell stock to someone at $32 if you could sell it in the open market for $40? In this example, the $0.50 put premium paid is the cost of the "insurance policy" that was never needed. It was as if you paid auto insurance premiums for a year and had no accidents.

If Silica-Corp declines to $30, the executive would exercise his put option and sell shares at $32. In this example, the $0.50 put premium paid protected the executive against $2 per share of loss. If Silica-Corp fell to $25 per share, the same option premium would have protected against $7 per share of loss.

Put options allow the executive to take a future unknown (the stock price) and purchase a "floor" for their shares.

ZERO-COST COLLARS

An executive might appreciate the downside protection of protective put options, but they might not like the cost required for that protection. In our previous example, the hypothetical put option cost $0.50 per share, or $5,000 to protect 10,000 shares. What if the executive wanted to protect 20,000 or 50,000 shares?

Would they be comfortable purchasing an "insurance policy" that would cost $10,000–$25,000?

There is a way to achieve the downside protection of the put option for potentially zero cost—by selling a call option against the shares simultaneously when a put option is purchased. The combination of these two options is known as a collar.

We know that a call option establishes a maximum stock price over a predetermined period, and the executive receives a cash premium by selling that option. The executive can then use the cash generated from the call option to pay for the put option. If the compensation received for the call option is equal to or greater than the premium required for the put option, there is no cost for this collar.

If you combine our two previous examples, an executive could sell a call option limiting their upside to $38 per share and, in exchange, receive a $0.50 per share cash premium. They could then use that cash to purchase a put option setting a minimum price of $32 per share.

The executive has now placed a "collar" around their shares. Without the option collar, the range of potential outcomes for Silica-Corp's stock price is $0 on the downside to infinity on the upside. With the option collar, the executive has narrowed possible outcomes to a minimum of $32 to a maximum of $38 per share until the options' expiration date.

SUBSTITUTE OR PROXY SECURITIES

We know that some companies have anti-hedging policies in place that prohibit their Section 16 officers from utilizing put or call options tied to their company shares.

If an executive is prohibited from hedging the risk of their own company, they might be able to find a competitor within their industry whose stock trades in a similar pattern to their own company. This stock alternative is known as a substitute or proxy security.

Delta Air Lines may prohibit their Section 16 officers from trading in Delta put or call options, but what if they used Southwest Airlines options? A Home Depot executive might look at Lowes, or an AT&T executive could consider Verizon.

If your company is part of a large industry, there might be an exchange-traded fund (ETF) that tracks your entire sector. There are ETFs that track the technology, energy, automobile, defense, pharmaceutical sectors, and so forth. Many ETFs have put and call options available on their shares.

Most substitute securities will not move in an identical pattern to the original security, but a good substitute will capture a large percentage of the original security's movement.

BE CAREFUL

In our examples of put options, call options, and zero-cost collars, the executive's trades are "covered" because they own the underlying shares committed via the options.

If you are trading in options of a substitute or proxy security, you would not own the substitute company's underlying shares. Without substitute share ownership, the option positions would be "naked" and subject to qualification requirements at the brokerage firm accepting the trades. You should also review additional risk mitigation techniques to guard against the price movement of the proxy security becoming too detached from your reference security.

If Delta's stock declines because of a health-related travel ban, Southwest's stock should also decrease. If Delta declines because of an accounting scandal or something not related to the risk of the entire industry, those substitute securities might move by a much smaller amount or not at all.

MINDFUL OF THE OPTICS

Remember our story about Sarah at the grocery store in our last chapter? Even though you might be compliant with your company's policies related to hedging, you should still proceed with caution. Your trades might follow the "letter of the law," but are you in compliance with the "spirit of the law"?

Any hedging that reduces your risk relative to regular shareholders means your interests are no longer perfectly aligned with the other shareholders. You might be able to defend your trades if questioned by the SEC, but would you be able to defend them at the grocery store if you were profiled in another local newspaper article?

For some Section 16 officers, their employer's policies will limit the amount of stock risk they can hedge away. In our next chapter, we will review other types of risks and threats that executives and their families can mitigate through traditional insurance.

CHAPTER 8

INSURE WHAT YOU CAN

"Plan ahead: It wasn't raining when Noah built the ark."

—RICHARD CUSHING

Tom and Sarah are feeling good about their progress thus far. They have been exercising employee options regularly, selling their restricted shares when released, and they periodically implement a 10b5-1 trading plan to set predetermined trigger points to reduce their Silica-Corp shares. Despite the wealth they are accumulating and amplifying, they have a nagging feeling that something is missing, and they are right.

What would happen to their long-term goals if Tom were unable to work due to a disability? What if Tom died before retirement? What if someone sued Tom and Sarah? Any one of those occurrences could derail an otherwise sound financial plan.

There is a solution: Insure what you can.

Many people have a love-hate relationship with the insurance industry. They love the idea of protecting their families, but they hate the process involved with getting that protection. It is not fun dealing with insurance agents, answering medical questions, having blood drawn for tests, and so on.

Let us look at the three areas of most significant risk for Tom and Sarah.

WHAT IF TOM DIES?

No one likes to think about their mortality. It is difficult to picture your family's struggles when you are gone. It's also nearly impossible to plan for the *emotional* assistance they will need. What is relatively easy to prepare for is the *financial* assistance required by your family after your death.

If planning for premature death is relatively easy, why do so many families suffer after the primary wage earner's passing? The answer is that many families cannot picture a life that is different from today, and that keeps them from making decisions about the future. Most humans have temporal myopia.

TEMPORAL MYOPIA

Our brains have a built-in bias to focus on immediate gratification, and temporal myopia is the inability to see ourselves in the future. For our ancestors, life was shorter and much less predictable. There were little or no cures for disease, less shelter from the elements, and food was only as bountiful as the hunters or gatherers could provide. Early man needed to live day by day. There was no ability to look toward the future or plan for the long term. Temporal myopia is an evolutionary inherited bias affecting our decisions in the present day.

Silica-Corp provides Tom a life insurance benefit of $936,000, equal to two times his base salary of $468,000. That is a large sum of money, but it would not provide a significant income stream for Sarah and the children. In fact, as a percentage of Tom's target compensation of $1.7 million, his company-paid life insurance benefit is only about half of one year's earnings.

Tom thought that Sarah and the children "could survive" with $936,000 of insurance benefits when added on top of their existing net worth of approximately $7 million. Sarah would also be entitled to 50 percent of Tom's future pension payments.

I agreed that the family's level of assets would be substantial, but should the goal be for the family to "survive," or should the goal be that they would have the same financial resources available when Tom was working? I think Tom's temporal myopia made it difficult for him to see a future for his family that did not include him.

To help make the future a bit clearer for Tom, I walked him through the following exercise.

"Tom, can you remember an instance when a professional athlete's contract was bought out? Sometimes teams feel it is more beneficial to pay a player a lump sum of money to 'go away' rather than keep them as part of the organization," I asked.

"I'm familiar with the concept," said Tom.

"How would you react if Silica-Corp approached you and offered to buy you out?"

This buyout was a hypothetical example, and Tom gave the answer everyone gives when asked this question: "My company would never offer that."

I pressed Tom a bit and said, "Let us suppose they *did* offer something like that. Would you consider it?"

"I guess so, but it would depend on how much cash they offered," he answered. His response to this question was also familiar.

"Would you consider walking away from Silica-Corp for a $1 million cash payment?" I asked.

Tom did not hesitate. He shook his head immediately and said, "No way. I like what I do, and I should earn five to ten times that amount over the next few years."

I then asked if he would accept a buyout of $5 million. Tom took a little bit longer to answer.

"Five million is a lot of money, and to have that available in a lump sum would be attractive."

Tom said he would have to investigate the job market, and if he felt he could get a job somewhere else within a year or two, he might consider a $5 million buyout.

"There is a catch to the $5 million," I told Tom. "If you accept it, Silica-Corp will require you to sign a lifetime noncompete agreement. In other words, once you receive the $5 million, you will never be able to work again."

"If that were the case, I wouldn't take it. I am only 55, and even if I work for only another five years, I would most likely earn substantially more than $5 million."

"If you wouldn't walk away from Silica-Corp for $5 million today," I continued, "what would it take for you to walk away, knowing you couldn't work again, and it would be the last paycheck you would ever receive?"

Tom thought for a while. "It would probably take $10 million for me to be comfortable with never working again." He quickly followed that up with, "But Silica-Corp would never offer me something like that."

I agreed that the likelihood of Silica-Corp writing Tom a check for $10 million to stay home was slim. But if that is what it would take for him to give up his current income stream, why would he let his family lose his income stream in exchange for $936,000 of life insurance benefits?

Tom paused and then nodded in agreement. His temporal myopia, his inability to see himself in the future, was altered. There is no way he would voluntarily exchange his current earnings for just $936,000 of cash, so why should he leave his family in that same position?

HOW MUCH LIFE INSURANCE IS NEEDED?

Tom said it would take $10 million to walk away from Silica-

Corp. That does not mean $10 million is the appropriate amount of life insurance, but it is a much better number than his company-provided benefit of $936,000.

When most people think of life insurance, they think about their family's needs in the immediate aftermath of their death—temporal myopia again. They want to make sure their family can stay in their home, so they want enough insurance to pay off their mortgage. They want to make sure their children will have enough money to go to college, so they want all future education expenses funded. They want to make sure there is enough money "leftover" for their spouse—but how is that amount defined? The mortgage is a known amount and so are college expenses (if you estimate high). It is easy to plan for known amounts.

What about open-ended obligations, such as the retirement income needed for their spouse? Sarah does not currently work outside of their home, and at Tom's passing, she will effectively be retired. Is the planning goal for Sarah to remain retired for the rest of her life, or will she have to leave retirement and reenter the workforce for a certain number of years?

It is never an issue of whether a spouse *can* reenter the workforce. Most spouses of Section 16 officers gave up lucrative careers to stay at home with their children. The decision to make is, should Sarah *have* to reenter the workforce, or should it be a choice?

Tom could provide enough insurance so Sarah could stay home with the children for a few years or until they are in college. Tom could also provide enough insurance so Sarah is never required to go back to work. With enough insurance or assets, if Sarah decided to reenter the workforce, it would be for nonmonetary reasons. She might want to volunteer or work in a fulfilling career that is not financially lucrative. It would be nice for her to have a choice.

Tom plans to work for several more years, contribute to his 401(k) and other savings plans, and receive a sizable pension from Silica-Corp.

These are the assumptions we use to estimate Tom and Sarah's future retirement income:

- If Tom works for a few more years and lives to retirement, he will save enough to provide for Sarah and him for the next forty years. He can also select a survivorship option on his pension, as high as a 100 percent joint annuity, so that payments will continue for Sarah if he predeceases her during retirement.
- If Tom dies before retirement, his ability to make those future retirement contributions, and select the 100 percent pension survivorship option, die with him.
- If the goal is to ensure Sarah can retire with the same lifestyle that Tom and Sarah were hoping to share as a couple, then Tom's life insurance should account for his future retirement savings (or lack thereof).

I think of life insurance as *"renting a net worth you hope to own in the future."* If Tom's goal was to accumulate $15 million of assets before retirement (excluding any pension benefits), and he has $7 million of investments today, plus $936,000 of existing life insurance benefits, then life insurance of approximately $7 million would seem appropriate. Tom can "rent" this $7 million of additional assets via insurance until the time he "owns" the assets in the future. This $7 million, plus the $936,000 of existing life insurance, is not too far away from the $10 million that Tom said it would take for him to accept a lump-sum buyout from Silica-Corp, never to work again.

There are many unknowns in life, but life insurance can solve the unknowns surrounding premature death. When you take the emotion out of a conversation about death, all that is left is a math problem.

How much will it cost today to make sure my family is taken care of in the future?

For Tom, $7 million of term insurance is relatively inexpensive as a percentage of his income.

A $7 million term insurance policy that will last for ten years will cost approximately $12,000 annually (based on Tom's age and good health). As a percentage of his target compensation of $1.7 million, this cost is less than 1 percent of his annual earnings. An insurance premium of $1,000 per month might seem high, but it is a small price to pay to know that Tom's family is taken care of between now and his retirement.

Why would we suggest a ten-year policy? Tom is 55 years old and plans to retire by the time he is 65 years old. His annual retirement and investment contributions, plus the growth of his existing assets, should total more than $7 million within the next ten years. He is *renting* the net worth he hopes to *own* by age 65. Once he has achieved that level of assets, the insurance is no longer necessary.

PERMANENT OR TEMPORARY INSURANCE?

The previous example of $7 million of life insurance for an annual premium of $12,000 is an example of *term insurance*—insurance designed to cover you for a particular term. Term insurance is always temporary since it will expire at the end of the agreed-upon term.

Some policies are permanent. *Permanent policies*, such as *whole life* policies, provide coverage that never expires, if you pay the required premium. If you die at age 95 or 105 and have continually paid your policy premium, your family receives the policy death benefit.

Suppose you could choose between a policy that will always pay a benefit (permanent) and one that will pay only during a specific period (term). Why would anyone select term insurance?

Although term policies expire after the agreed-upon term, that is precisely the purpose of those policies. They are the purest form of insurance and therefore the least costly. If Tom were to purchase a $7 million whole life policy (permanent insurance), the required premium could be in the $100,000–$200,000 range each year.

Insurance agents will often sell another feature of permanent policies—the policy's ability to accumulate a cash value accessible before death. The cash value is a nice benefit, but it is rarely worth the considerable premium increase compared to the term insurance cost.

There are some instances where permanent insurance policies might be required, such as paying future estate taxes or business buy-sell agreements. Review your unique needs with your licensed life insurance agent.

My recommendation is to utilize term insurance whenever possible.

Rent the net worth you hope to own by the expiration date of the term policy.

WHAT ABOUT SARAH?

A typical financial planning mistake is insuring the family's primary wage earner but neglecting to insure their spouse. Families justify that decision if the spouse's earnings are significantly less than the primary wage earner.

In Tom and Sarah's case, Sarah stays home with the children, contributing no wages to the family. Does that mean there would not be a financial burden if she were no longer available to do her job? Absolutely not.

Like most families, Tom and Sarah's children are always on the go. From soccer practice to Boy Scouts, choir rehearsal to gymnastics, and robotics club to karate, Sarah coordinates these activities for the children daily. There are in-school events and after-school events, doctor appointments, dentist appointments, eye-care appointments, automobile repairs, home repairs, homework and study time for the children, meal planning, grocery shopping, and meal preparation. The list goes on.

Salary.com prepared a list of job duties required for stay-at-home spouses, including:

- Accountant
- Dietitian
- Facilities Director
- Groundskeeper
- Interior Designer
- Maintenance Supervisor
- Child Psychologist
- Nurse
- Tailor
- Tutor

To name a few. The average stay-at-home spouse works ninety-six hours per week performing these different duties to support their family.

Tom has had an incredible career with Silica-Corp, but it has not come without sacrifice. There are many days each month when Tom is required to travel out of town. It might be a short two-day trip to an investor meeting in New York City, or it might be a two-week tour of multiple plants in China. Even on days when Tom is working locally, he might have a dinner meeting with vendors or customers and not make it home until late. Perhaps Tom is home for dinner but then has a conference call with employees in South Korea at 9:00 p.m. US time (morning in South Korea).

Sarah is the one at home picking up the slack during Tom's absence. It is their shared sacrifice.

Imagine what their lives would look like if Sarah passed while the children were still young.

- Would Tom be able to leave work in the mid-afternoon to shuttle the kids to their activities?
- Would he be able to take a couple of hours off to meet the house painter and get the quote for the work needed?
- Can Tom eliminate all meetings after 5:00 p.m. to be home to cook dinner?

Tom could make those schedule changes, but doing so would most likely require him to move to a different position in Silica-Corp, one with fewer responsibilities and therefore less compensation.

When we consider all the different duties Sarah performs for the family and knowing it is Sarah's work at home that allows Tom to excel in his position at Silica-Corp, we can calculate a specific financial loss if Sarah were to pass away.

At Sarah's passing, Tom will face the choice of changing his career path with Silica-Corp to free up his schedule or hiring help for the family. Either way, there is a cost if Sarah is gone.

Salary.com estimates that 100 percent of a stay-at-home spouse's duties would cost $163,000 to hire out. Tom might not want to hire assistance for all those duties, but he may need help with a large portion of them. If Tom requires assistance with half of those jobs at a cost of $80,000 annually, the expense over ten years would be $800,000.

Sarah might not need $800,000 of life insurance because the net present value of $800,000 over ten years would be less today and some expenses might go down as the children get older and become more self-sufficient. Regardless of the assumptions used, if Sarah were to die while the children were still at home, the family would suffer a significant financial loss.

TOM BECOMES DISABLED

When Section 16 officers think of risk, early death is at the top of their list. However, the risk of a lengthy or permanent disability can be just as damaging to their family's financial future.

According to the Social Security Administration, 10 million citizens received disability benefits in 2018. It is exceedingly challenging to qualify for Social Security disability benefits, and for those who *do* qualify, the average monthly payment is only $1,200.

Silica-Corp offers a disability policy to all employees. The short-term benefit provides a payment equal to 100 percent of Tom's base salary for the first six months of any covered disability. If Tom were to be disabled for more than six months, the long-term benefit provides 50 percent of Tom's base salary up until he is 65 years old. The maximum payment from Silica-Corp's long-term disability plan is $15,000 per month.

Fifty percent of Tom's $468,000 base salary is $234,000 annually, which is $19,500 per month. Silica-Corp caps Tom's benefit at $15,000 per month or $180,000 annually. Although this is a sizable sum, it disappears at age 65. Also, Silica-Corp's disability plan does not cover any bonus compensation or stock-based compensation. Tom's target compensation, including bonuses and long-term incentives, is $1.7 million annually, so the $180,000 disability benefit covers just over 10 percent of his target compensation.

If Tom were to become disabled, $180,000 is enough to cover most of their everyday household expenses, but what about continuing to save for future college tuition expenses? What about saving for retirement? Tom would not be accruing retirement benefits in Silica-Corp's pension plan when receiving disability benefits.

WHAT IS THE SOLUTION?

Tom can purchase a *private disability policy* to supplement his Silica-Corp plan. Most private plans will allow Tom to insure up to 60 percent of his total compensation, not just his base salary.

A private plan remains in force, independent of your status with your employer. Silica-Corp might decide to terminate its company-sponsored disability plan. Likewise, you might change employers throughout your career, and perhaps your new employer does not offer a disability plan. With a private plan, you are in control of your benefits.

One of the most lucrative benefits of a private disability policy is the taxation of future benefits. If you pay for the policy with after-tax dollars, any benefits received from the policy are income tax-free.

Given Tom's federal and state income tax bracket, he would only need to cover approximately 55 percent of his total compensation to generate the same take-home pay he receives from Silica-Corp.

PLANNING TIP

As an alternative to private insurance, your employer might offer you the ability to purchase supplemental disability coverage *in addition* to the standard employee benefit. If available, make sure you pay for that coverage with after-tax dollars. After-tax premiums qualify future benefits received from the policy as tax-free income. Collecting benefits tax-free will provide a significant financial boost over the months or years you are disabled.

Most employers default to pretax contributions for benefit programs. You may have to ask to have your disability premiums paid with after-tax dollars.

TOM IS SUED

We live in a litigious society, and Tom and Sarah (and their family) are a good target for lawsuits. Tom has a high-profile position with Silica-Corp, and his name is in the newspaper frequently whenever he sells company stock. The value of his stock holdings is public record, giving anyone the ability to estimate his net worth.

We have all heard stories about outlandish, frivolous lawsuits, defined as not having any serious purpose or value. Here is my favorite:

OVERTON V. ANHEUSER-BUSCH CO.

In 1993, the makers of Budweiser beer were sued by a customer for false advertising. Richard Overton claimed that he drank a six-pack of Bud Light, and the beer failed to produce a group of beautiful women on a beach as suggested by Budweiser's advertising campaign. He sued for $10,000 of damages due to emotional distress brought on by their deceptive marketing.

It is hard not to laugh when reading that claim. The court agreed and dismissed the case. Even though Anheuser-Busch prevailed, they still had to go through the time and expense of defending themselves against that frivolous lawsuit.

Not all lawsuits are frivolous. What if Tom were to get in a car accident, and the other driver had substantial medical bills and was out of work for six months? If someone with a modest net worth was responsible for the accident, any lawsuit might end with a request for medical bills and lost wages reimbursement. If Tom was involved, the suit might request a significant settlement to cover the "pain and suffering" the victim endured, well above their medical expenses and lost wages. Tom is a good target.

HOW CAN TOM AND SARAH PROTECT THEMSELVES?

You have probably never heard of *lawsuit insurance*, but that is the primary role of excess personal liability insurance, commonly referred to as *umbrella insurance*. Umbrella insurance picks up where the liability portion of your auto and homeowner's insurance ends.

Most auto and homeowner's insurance policies have liability limits of $100,000–$300,000. If you were sued for a car accident and ordered to pay $1 million, you would be responsible for any award above your policy limits. Umbrella insurance would cover that excess liability, so you would not need to liquidate assets to pay the judgment.

Umbrella insurance is for more than just auto accidents. You can think of it as "family lawsuit protection insurance."

Here are some examples where Tom and Sarah's assets could be at risk through the actions of their family members:

- Tom and Sarah's eighth-grade son invites a friend over after school. The children are wrestling with the family dog, and the dog gets overly excited and bites the friend. The friend needs a trip to the emergency room for stitches but otherwise is okay. Tom and Sarah get sued for the other family's medical expenses and the pain, suffering, and mental anguish the animal attack caused the child. The lawsuit seeks $1 million.
- Sarah volunteers to be a chaperone on a trip for their tenth-grade daughter's class—the class is visiting Washington, DC, and spending the night. A student sneaked alcohol into the hotel, and four students were drinking. Sarah's daughter was not involved. One of the students who was drinking slipped and hit their head, requiring a trip to the emergency room. The student suffered a concussion, and a large gash on their

forehead required plastic surgery. The student now has trouble concentrating in school, and their grades have suffered. Despite the plastic surgery, the student has a visible scar. Sarah and the other chaperones receive notice of a $3 million lawsuit, claiming they failed to supervise and protect the students.

- Tom and Sarah's son in eleventh grade always seems to butt heads with his soccer coach. The coach is also his math teacher. The coach frequently yells at players, and some of the players start spreading rumors about the coach on social media. Tom and Sarah's son is not the source of any rumors, but he participates in the "online bashing" by forwarding and reposting the claims. Even though the stories are not true, the issue is embarrassing for both the coach and the school. The school ultimately fires the coach, and the coach sues Tom and Sarah for $4 million, claiming their son's "online misinformation campaign" cost him his job. The coach also claims he cannot find new employment because the rumors appear attached to his name in Google search results.

EXAMINE YOUR COVERAGE

Not all policies will cover the same risks. Please make sure to review your coverage with your insurance agent for specific details on coverage and exclusions.

Most parents believe their children would never *intentionally* bring financial harm to the family, and they would be right. The trouble is the harm resulting from *unintentional* behavior or others' behavior. You do not want a single dog bite from an otherwise loving family pet to reduce your retirement assets by $1 million or more. An umbrella policy can help reduce this risk.

A large umbrella policy provides an additional benefit of aligning the insurance company's interests with your interests. Most policies have a *duty to defend clause* requiring the insurance company to defend you against liability lawsuits. If the insurance company faces a maximum exposure of $100,000 from your auto or homeowner's insurance, they will provide you with a legal team capable of protecting their $100,000 risk. Suppose the insurance company could lose $5 million, the theoretical limit of your umbrella policy. In that case, the insurance company will likely provide you a legal team better suited to protect their more considerable exposure.

PLANNING TIP

Umbrella insurance is inexpensive relative to the coverage it provides. Most families can purchase a policy covering $3 million of excess liability coverage for $400–$600 annually. A $5 million policy might cost $600–$1,000 annually. This premium is a small cost for the peace of mind these policies provide.

Tom and Sarah appreciate the *Guidance* provided by the first pillar of the *Section 16 GPS* process. Their net worth is increasing, and they regularly reduce their exposure to Silica-Corp. They have insured their family in case of death, disability, or lawsuits and feel confident about their progress.

Tom and Sarah also recognize that the rewards from Tom's position with Silica-Corp make them more financially successful and comfortable than most people in the world. Now Tom and Sarah want to support causes meaningful to them. We will also explore ways that Tom and Sarah can get their children involved in their giving to help pass on their charitable mindset to the next generation.

In our next chapter, we will move on to the second pillar of the *Section 16 GPS* process, **Philanthropy**, and review charitable and philanthropic strategies.

CHAPTER 9

CHARITABLE GIVING

TAX EFFICIENCY, FAMILY LEGACY, AND IMPACT GIVING

"We make a living by what we get, but we make a life by what we give."

—WINSTON CHURCHILL

The next pillar of the *Section 16 GPS* process is **Philanthropy.**

Tom and Sarah never considered themselves "philanthropists." They have always supported various charities but never via a well-thought-out plan. They write checks to a handful of charities each year, and sometimes they make credit card donations to accumulate frequent-flyer miles. Occasionally, they will send money to "one-off" charities after receiving solicitations in the mail. Despite not having a formal giving plan, they have consistently gifted $25,000–$50,000 annually to various charities.

Tom and Sarah feel they are ready to increase and enhance

their charitable giving, so this chapter will review philanthropic strategies. Equally important, we will examine ways to share Tom and Sarah's generous mindset with their children.

TAX EFFICIENCY

When most people think about tax efficiency related to charitable giving, they think of their tax deduction received. If they gift $10,000 to United Way, for example, they reduce their taxable income by $10,000, resulting in less tax liability for the year.

For some taxpayers, that deduction could be worth 44 percent or more of the amount donated (assuming a 37 percent federal income tax bracket and a 7 percent state income tax bracket). A $10,000 donation could potentially save $4,400 of income taxes. A $100,000 gift could save $44,000 of income taxes.

The income tax savings from charitable donations represent only a portion of the total tax savings available. Additional tax benefits materialize based on the "currency" you use to make your donation.

If you make your donation by writing a check or using a credit card, you are using after-tax dollars. If you make your donation using appreciated stock or using IRA assets, you amplify your gift using pretax dollars eligible for additional tax savings.

APPRECIATED STOCK

When you gift shares of stock to a charity, you are not only gifting the current market value of the shares; you also transfer the cost basis of that security to the charity.

For example, suppose you purchased one hundred shares of XYZ stock at $50 per share a decade ago, for a total cost of $5,000. Today, XYZ stock is trading at $100 per share, so your one hundred shares are worth $10,000.

If you gift those one hundred shares to a charity, the charity receives $10,000 worth of stock with a cost basis of $5,000. The charity can immediately sell the shares to convert the one hundred shares of stock into $10,000 of cash. Even though the charity sold shares at a $5,000 profit, the charity does not realize the capital gain nor pays any capital gains taxes because the charity is a tax-exempt organization.

As the donor, you do not realize any capital gain either because you did not sell the shares—the charity did. By gifting shares of appreciated stock instead of cash, you have removed a future capital gain from your portfolio. The additional tax savings generated by giving appreciated securities can be significant.

Let us assume Tom and Sarah wish to gift $100,000 to various charities this year.

With a combined federal and state tax bracket of 44 percent, a $100,000 cash gift will generate tax savings of $44,000 for Tom and Sarah.

Alternatively, Tom and Sarah could gift $100,000 of appreciated stock. They can transfer securities with a 150 percent unrealized capital gain to the charities. Their cost basis in these shares is $40,000, and the market value is $100,000. If Tom and Sarah were to sell these shares themselves and realize a $60,000 long-term capital gain, their tax burden would be approximately

$18,500 (federal capital gains tax, state income tax, and Affordable Care Act excise tax).

By utilizing appreciated securities for their gift, their total current and future tax savings is more than 62 percent of the amount donated.

GIFTING APPRECIATED STOCK

Market Value of Stock Gift: $100,000

Cost Basis of Stock Gift: $40,000

Future Capital Gain Removed: $60,000

Current Income Tax Savings on Gift: $44,000

Future Capital Gains/ACA Tax Savings: $18,500

Total Tax Savings: $62,500

You should review the strategy of gifting appreciated securities with your tax preparer or CPA. Only after-tax securities owned for more than a year will qualify for the special tax treatment referenced above. If you gift securities owned for *less* than a year, you cannot claim the stock's market value as your charitable donation and would be limited to claiming your cost basis (the amount you paid for the stock).

DONOR ADVISED FUND

My favorite way to gift appreciated securities is by utilizing a donor advised fund (DAF).

You might be familiar with *Christmas club accounts*—special saving accounts offered by banks and credit unions where savers can fund the account throughout the year, putting aside money to spend on holiday shopping. Or you may have established other special savings accounts in the past, such as a "vacation account" or a "new car account." Think of a DAF as a *charitable gift savings account*. You fund this account to distribute charitable gifts in the future.

A DAF is a registered charity established by a nonprofit organization. Donors make an irrevocable gift of cash or appreciated securities into the DAF to be distributed later to a charity of their choice. Because the fund itself is a registered charity, donors receive an immediate tax deduction for their contribution. They do not have to wait to distribute their gift to the final charity to claim their deduction.

Donors can invest contributions to a DAF in mutual funds or other securities, and if the account value grows, they can gift the profits to their chosen charities as well. Of course, if the account value falls, the donor will have less to give.

The donor's tax deduction is based on the shares' value when received by the DAF and future appreciation (or depreciation) does not impact the tax deduction.

The largest sponsors of DAF include Charles Schwab, Fidelity, and Vanguard.

WHAT ARE THE BENEFITS OF A DAF?

The benefits of a DAF are extensive. You get an immediate tax deduction for gifts to a DAF, even if you do not distribute any money to a final charity right away. You can make a gift to a DAF today and allow it to grow tax-free over time before making a grant to your selected charity (subject to any accumulation rules of the fund).

We previously reviewed the benefits of gifting appreciated securities directly to a charity, and you can do the same thing with a DAF. A gift of appreciated securities eliminates a future capital gain from your portfolio, and assets held within a DAF are not subject to estate taxes at your passing.

You can provide a custom name for your DAF, such as The Tom and Sarah Smith Charitable Fund.

DAFs' internal investment expenses are usually low, and any costs are significantly less than establishing a private foundation.

WHAT ARE THE DOWNSIDES?

There are a few to consider. For example, your gift to the DAF is irrevocable. Once you make a gift to the DAF, you no longer control the money. Your role becomes one of a "nominator"— you instruct the DAF when to grant (distribute) money to your selected charities.

Because you are a nominator and not the owner, there is always a risk the DAF denies your request to support a particular charity. I have never seen a request to give to an established 501(c) (3) charity denied, but if you wish to support a newly formed charity, I suggest speaking with the DAF sponsor to get the new charity "approved" before making your contribution to the DAF.

There are other items to consider, so please make sure you speak directly with a DAF sponsor before donating. Also, consult with your tax preparer or advisor before making any irrevocable donations.

WHY NOT GIVE DIRECTLY TO A CHARITY?

Many of our clients ask us why they cannot donate to a charity themselves. Some smaller charities might not have a brokerage account established and cannot accept appreciated stock gifts directly. Your DAF converts your stock donation to cash for the charity and sends them a check.

You might like to support some charities over multiple months or years. Rather than give all the money to the charity up front, you can donate to your DAF in a lump sum and then have the DAF distribute grants to your selected charity over time.

Also, you might like to donate anonymously to a charity. With a DAF, you can withhold your name from the end charity. Tom and Sarah already deal with public disclosure of their activity with Silica-Corp shares, so sometimes they do not want their names linked to a certain level of giving in a charity's annual list of donors.

REAL-LIFE STORIES

We have assisted many clients with DAF over the past two decades. Here are three real-life scenarios where the funds have been helpful.

ACCELERATED GIFTS IN A HEFTY TAX YEAR

We had a Section 16 client who received a substantial seven-figure bonus. Knowing he would have a big tax bill that year, we placed several hundred thousand dollars in a DAF before the end of the year. The client received an immediate tax deduction, and he "prefunded" his charitable donations for many years to come.

ACCELERATED GIFTS BEFORE CHANGES IN TAX LAW

Congress passed tax cuts in December 2017, effective for 2018. We assisted many clients with accelerated gifts to their DAF before the end of 2017. The highest federal tax bracket fell from 39.6 percent in 2017 to 37 percent in 2018. By accelerating their gifts in 2017, clients in the highest tax bracket received an additional 2.6 percent tax savings.

AUTOPILOT FOR SNOWBIRDS

We have many clients who travel south for the winter, but they wish to continue supporting their local church on a month-to-month basis. Rather than have the burden of mailing checks in the winter months or making annual contributions to their church, a DAF can mail a check for a predetermined amount every month (or even every week). A donor can make an annual gift of stock to the DAF, and then the DAF can send out a regular donation to an end charity on a preselected schedule.

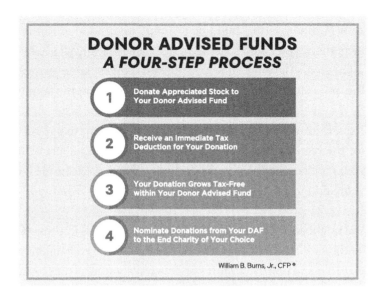

DONOR ADVISED FUNDS
A FOUR-STEP PROCESS

1. Donate Appreciated Stock to Your Donor Advised Fund
2. Receive an Immediate Tax Deduction for Your Donation
3. Your Donation Grows Tax-Free within Your Donor Advised Fund
4. Nominate Donations from Your DAF to the End Charity of Your Choice

William B. Burns, Jr., CFP ®

FAMILY LEGACY: GET THE FAMILY INVOLVED

We have reviewed ways to make charitable gifts more tax efficient, but for most people, tax savings are just a tiny part of their reason for giving. I believe most of our clients would continue their gifting programs even if the tax benefits went away.

Many families are not concerned about the risk of tax benefits diminishing but fear the next generation might not remain as charitably minded as mom and dad. For Tom and Sarah, we worked on getting their children more involved in their charitable giving to help pass on their charitable mindset to the next generation.

FAMILY MEETINGS

Tom and Sarah set time aside each year to include their children in the decision-making process about the charities they support.

Your family meeting could be a simple discussion at dinner, or perhaps you could schedule a dedicated "family charitable discussion." The more effort you put into the discussion process, the more attention you will receive from the rest of the family.

Explain to your children what charities you plan to support for the year, and if you are comfortable sharing numbers with your children, let them know the budget you have set aside for your support.

You might also decide to budget a certain amount to be directed by the children. You could ask the children to research different charities and prepare a short presentation about why the family should support a particular one.

For young children, their presentation might focus on their feelings about the charity's mission. For older children and young adults, you could ask them to study the charity's annual report and review where their dollars could have the most impact. They could also research the fiscal responsibility of the charity at www.charitynavigator.org.

$250 GIFT VOUCHER

For the Charity of your Choice

Suppose you did not want to formalize the charitable process with a family meeting. In that case, you could give a gift certificate to your children (or grandchildren) referencing a dollar amount for them to give away during the year.

A $250 charitable gift certificate (or $100, or $10,000—whatever works for your family) could be donated in a lump sum or split up among multiple charities.

CHARITABLE CHALLENGE

Another idea is to structure a *charitable challenge* with the children. Give them a budget and ask them to find ways to leverage their gift to "make a bigger impact."

"If you give a man a fish, you feed him for a day. Teach a man to fish, and you feed him for a lifetime."

—CHINESE PROVERB

Tom and Sarah provide their children with a "charity budget" of $1,000 annually, and each year during their family meeting, they assist their teenage children with brainstorming ideas for the coming year to better leverage their giving.

To organize a food drive for the local food pantry, one year they used $100 of their budget to print 2,000 flyers to distribute in their community. They delivered a flyer to each home in their town on a Saturday, telling their neighbors they would be back the *following* Saturday to pick up the food items. They also spent $600 on a Facebook advertising campaign targeting their local community to get the word out about the food drive and ask for additional volunteers. With the remaining $300 of their budget, they rented two U-Haul trucks to collect the donations to deliver to the food pantry.

Another year, the children spent several months collecting coupons for various food items. Rather than donating cash to the food pantry, the children used the coupons, did the shopping themselves, and leveraged their $1,000 budget to purchase more food to donate.

In the future, they have plans to utilize $1,000 to cultivate a vegetable garden in their backyard. A garden could provide an ongoing supply of fresh vegetables to the local food pantry. Sarah has always had an interest in horticulture and is excited to help.

Some year, at the end of the winter season in March, they have plans to spend $1,000 to purchase winter clothes. They will find better deals as stores start to make room for their summer inventory, and they will save the items for donation to homeless shelters in the fall. To further leverage the volume they can donate, they plan to purchase the clothing at secondhand stores.

IMPACT GIVING

As Tom and Sarah have become more comfortable with their charitable giving, we started discussing ways for their gifts to have a more significant impact on the world around them.

Impact giving is a strategy employed to try to ensure your charitable dollars are having a bigger "impact" and effecting the change in the world you would like to see. Impact giving is the heart of philanthropy. Philanthropists focus their efforts on solving problems over several years, whereas charitable donations tend to focus on immediate relief for different organizations.

Many people contribute annually to the "general fund" of different charities. They trust that the charities will use the money wherever it is needed most. For many donors and donation amounts, this is a perfectly appropriate strategy.

As the value of your donation increases and if you can commit to a multiyear donation, you have the opportunity to more closely scrutinize the impact your donation is making.

What if you could donate $100,000 to a particular charity in a single year? What if you could commit to a $50,000 donation annually for the next five years, for a total of $250,000? Would you still be comfortable supporting the "general fund" of that charity?

IMPACT GIVING

Work with your chosen charity on a specific measurable goal. Offer to fund the goal over a period of years, with a well-defined set of success criteria to be met along the way. Become a partner in that success by offering your unique business skills in addition to your financial support.

Impact givers collaborate with charities to solve a specific and well-defined problem. For example, the goal of "ending homelessness" is overly broad, and there may not be enough money in the world to meet that goal. The objective of reducing the number of homeless families in your community by 20 percent over the next five years is much more specific and perhaps more attainable.

An impact giver might formulate a proposal with homeless advocates and agencies on a five-year plan to hit that 20 percent goal. You might commit to a $50,000 annual budget over five years but with the stipulation that only the first three years or $150,000 is guaranteed. You could reserve the right to stop funding years four and five unless your charitable partners in this project have been able to quantify at least a 10 percent reduction in homelessness after three years. In other words, you link your donation to the actual success of the project.

Some donors are not interested in the time it takes to hold charities accountable. They want to give and move out of the way. For others, their financial support is just one part of the value they can bring to the charity. As part of the accountability process, an impact giver might offer their managerial skills to help the charity track their project's key metrics. An impact giver could speak at community events to raise additional funds for their mission. An impact giver becomes an integral part of the problem-solving team.

Tom and Sarah are grateful for their financial security. The monetary rewards from Tom's position with Silica-Corp allow them to support different charities to give back. They can also select one or two charities every decade to work with as an impact donor.

Although charities always need current gifts, Tom and Sarah also recognize that one of the most considerable gifts they can provide the world is to make sure they pass their charitable mindset on to their children. Hopefully, their children will then pass on that family value to subsequent generations.

Tom and Sarah are also concerned about what they can leave behind for the next generation(s). Most families desire to see their children, grandchildren, and great-grandchildren thrive and prosper. Tom and Sarah hope to live for many years to witness their family's success firsthand and hope they have accumulated enough to leave a portion of their estate behind for future generations, *after* funding their various philanthropic goals.

In our next chapter, we will explore opportunities for Tom and Sarah to steward a portion of their wealth to the next generation As we will review in the third pillar of the *Section 16 GPS* process, effective stewardship involves more than just financial assets.

CHAPTER 10

NEXT-GENERATION WEALTH TRANSFER

MORE THAN JUST FINANCIAL ASSETS

"All good men and women must take responsibility to create legacies that will take the next generation to a level we could only imagine."

—JIM ROHN

The last pillar of the *Section 16 GPS* process is **Stewardship.**

In biblical times, a "steward" was the "manager of a large household." Over time, the concept of stewardship has evolved to include responsibility for anything of value. Today, we are all stewards of both the financial and nonfinancial assets of our households.

How do we steward those assets to the next generation?

For many families, a simple will is all that is needed—a document that states that if one spouse dies, the other spouse inherits everything, and if both spouses die, the children inherit everything.

Tom and Sarah do not have a simple estate. Their current assets are worth over $7 million, and they expect their investments to be close to $15 million by the time Tom retires. If Tom dies before retirement, they have secured an $8 million life insurance policy, so their estate will still be close to $15 million.

It is beyond this book's scope to provide specific legal advice, but there are a handful of planning tools that might be appropriate for Tom and Sarah. You should make sure to review these tools with your legal counsel.

REVOCABLE TRUSTS

A *revocable living trust* allows Tom and Sarah to manage their assets as "trustees" instead of direct owners. They still retain the benefit of direct ownership, and as trustees, they could decide to "revoke" the trust at any time. Since they have that right to revoke, a revocable trust does not provide any estate tax savings, and it will not protect assets from nursing home expenses or other creditors.

The primary benefit of a revocable living trust is that at Tom or Sarah's passing, the assets in the trust do not need to pass through probate (a court proceeding to distribute your investments and belongings). Tom or Sarah can manage the trust assets just as they did before. When *both* Tom and Sarah have passed away, a successor trustee, predetermined by Tom and Sarah, steps in to distribute the assets to the children. Or perhaps the trust converts to an irrevocable trust to provide additional protections for the next generation.

A trust also provides Tom and Sarah, and their heirs, increased privacy. The assets of a trust are distributed in *private* by the trustees. If assets pass via a will, the will is made part of the public record during the probate process. Anyone has the right to examine a will at the clerk's office of the probate court.

Finally, a trust protects the family if Tom or Sarah becomes disabled. The trust document will name successor trustees to manage the trust assets if Tom or Sarah cannot do so. Successor trustees could be one or all of the children if they are adults, another family member, a close friend, or a corporate entity such as a bank.

IRREVOCABLE TRUSTS

Tom and Sarah could also choose to establish an *irrevocable living trust*. An irrevocable trust provides an added security layer for Tom and Sarah, but it comes at a cost. If a trust is irrevocable, Tom and Sarah cannot change the trust once funded or request the assets back.

Because the trust is irrevocable, the trust assets are typically safe from the claims of creditors. Suppose Tom or Sarah were sued and found liable for something, and the judgment was more than their umbrella insurance coverage. In that case, the court typically cannot look to assets in an irrevocable trust to satisfy the judgment. There are also estate planning and nursing home planning benefits if an irrevocable trust meets specific requirements.

Tom and Sarah might choose to establish *separate* irrevocable trusts for the benefit of their children. Tom and Sarah can gift assets each year into the trust for the children, and those assets will be free from the claims of creditors—both Tom and Sarah's creditors and the children's future creditors.

It might be strange to think of the children's future creditors, but they will be adults at some point. What if they were involved in a car accident? What if the children get married and then divorced? Creditors usually cannot seize money held in an irrevocable trust for the children's benefit.

SPECIALIZED TRUSTS

Suppose any of Tom or Sarah's children have special needs. In that case, they could implement an *irrevocable special needs trust*—a trust created so the government does not deny the children certain benefits. Since most government programs are income based, if a child with special needs inherits assets directly, the government could force them to spend those assets first before qualifying for other forms of assistance.

If Tom and Sarah are the direct owners of their life insurance policies, any policy proceeds paid at death are included in their estate for estate tax purposes. An *irrevocable life insurance trust* is a special trust designed to own a life insurance policy outside of your estate. Trust ownership of life insurance policies will reduce your taxable estate and will also protect the life insurance benefits from the beneficiaries' creditors.

PLANNING TIP

Think about your goals and objectives for the next generation of your family. Are you concerned with them inheriting a large amount of wealth outright with no restrictions? Are you concerned about the children's future creditors? Do you wish to keep information about your estate and beneficiaries private and not part of a probate proceeding? Think about these items and schedule a time to chat with an estate planning attorney.

Although trusts might be appropriate for some families, they are not suitable for *all* families. You should consult with your estate planning attorney before deciding to implement trusts into your estate plan. Do not base your decision after reading one chapter in this book—I am not an attorney. These ideas have been presented in a financial planning capacity only and should not be relied on as legal advice.

IS THERE ANYTHING ELSE?

You might think this chapter should end here. We have discussed some simple ways to steward and transfer financial assets to the next generation. Is there anything else? After all, when we think about assets, most people naturally think of **financial** assets. Stocks, bonds, mutual funds, cash, real estate, and business ventures are all significant assets that can be passed on to future generations, *but are these **all** your assets?*

Proper stewardship involves more than just financial assets.

What about your **knowledge and experience**? The knowledge and experience you have accumulated over your lifetime is also a family asset.

- What if you could help the next generation learn from your mistakes?
- What if you could teach them some of the skills you acquired that allowed you to succeed in the corporate world or as an entrepreneur?

Would you like the next generation to know about your **culture and avocations**?

- Are you a proud Irish American?
- Do you have stories to share of your grandparents or great-grandparents growing up in Greece and how they sacrificed to come to the United States?
- Do you practice a particular religious faith?
- What about your hobbies?
- Has sailing been a big part of your family history? Is teaching the next generation the rules of the water and how to sail important to you?
- Are you a musician who hopes your children and grandchildren will inherit, or at least appreciate, your musical talent?

How do you view your **core family values**, aka your ethics and sense of right and wrong?

- Is it important to pass those traits on?
- Do you have a charitable mindset?

- Do you try to leave the world a better place each day by supporting causes that are important to you?
- Do you dedicate yourself to thankfulness?
- Would you like to know that the next generation also appreciates the opportunities they have been given and are carrying on your charitable activities?
- Have you discussed a charitable legacy with your family?

All the "assets" reviewed above are beautiful gifts to be passed on to future generations, and in a perfect world, you could. How would your life or outlook change if you could *not* pass along all four categories of assets—financial, knowledge and experience, culture and avocations, and your core family values? What if you could pass along only two types? Could you choose?

If you could choose only two categories, most families would want to start with their financial assets. Future generations could benefit from the hard work and success of previous generations. Most families would also like to pass along the asset of their core family values, including their family ethics and charitable mindset. Any child or grandchild would be incredibly fortunate to receive those assets from you, even without the benefit of your knowledge, experience, cultural history, and hobbies.

Here comes the challenging part. *What if you could pass along only one asset?* What would you choose? Would you elect future generations to receive your financial wealth without knowing the core family values that allowed you to generate that wealth fairly and ethically? Would you feel you lived up to the definition of "successful" if future generations knew nothing of your core values, even if they inherited your financial assets?

Hopefully, no family needs to make this choice, and you can pass on everything that makes you "YOU." However, you should ask yourself:

- How much time have I spent cultivating my other assets to pass on? Is it an important goal for me?
- Have you spent time with your family talking about your formative years and why you selected your career?
- Do your children know of the successes and failures you encountered as a Section 16 corporate insider?
- How about spending time reviewing your heritage?
- Have you taken any trips to the birthplace of your grandparents or great-grandparents?
- Are your children included in the decision-making process for some of your charitable gifting?
- Do they know why you support specific causes?

We tend to spend a lot of time cultivating financial assets and teaching our children about money management principles. If our nonfinancial assets are essential to our lives, we need to spend time nurturing those ideals for future generations as well.

What do you want to pass on to the next generation?

In a perfect world, you would be able to pass on everything that makes you, "YOU." Give them your Financial Assets, your Knowledge and Experience, help them learn about your Culture, Religion, Hobbies, and Passions, and pass along your Ethics, Sense of Family, and a Charitable Mindset. But what if you could only pass them two categories?

What if you could only pass along one?

What is the most important and really makes you, "YOU"?

Financial Assets
- Stocks
- Mutual Funds
- Cash
- Real Estate
- Business Assets

Knowledge & Experience
- If I knew then what I know now
- Learn from my mistakes

YOU

Core Values
- Ethics
- Sense of Family
- Charitable Mindset
- Dedicate yourself to thankfulness

Cultural & Avocations
- National Heritage
- Faith & Religious Views
- Hobbies & Passions

William B. Burns, Jr., CFP®

THE FAMILY INTERVIEW

Here is an idea to help you nurture the other three family assets: knowledge and experience, culture and avocations, and core family values.

In a *family interview*, ask your children to prepare a list of questions to ask you. The interview can be video recorded, and then a transcript of the interview can be generated. The transcript can become the basis of a family history document passed down through the generations.

Family interview questions might include:

- What kind of work did your father do for a living? Did he have more than one profession?
- Do you have any special memories of your grandparents?
- What do you remember about your great-grandparents? Did you ever meet them?
- Can you describe your childhood home? Do you remember the address? Have you ever gone back to visit?
- What was your first job? Do you recall any ethical dilemmas you faced at that job, and how did you handle them?
- Do you have any memories of your parents or grandparents helping others?
- If you were given $1 million and had to give it away to various charities, what charities would you choose and why?

GET THE GRANDPARENTS INVOLVED

If your parents are still alive, your children can interview them as well. Your parents might have vivid memories of their grandparents (your great-grandparents) to gift to future generations.

Tom and Sarah were thankful for our discussion about stewardship of their financial and nonfinancial assets. They anticipate their children will inherit a decent-sized estate someday, and they never want them to "forget where they came from."

After reviewing the Guidance, Philanthropy, and Stewardship pillars of the *Section 16 GPS* process, Tom asked the question, "What's next?"

In the next chapter, we will review Tom's plan to someday retire from Silica-Corp. We know he is ready financially. Is he ready *mentally*?

PART 2

HEALTHSPAN EXTENDER

CHAPTER 11

RETIRE "TO" SOMETHING, NOT "FROM" SOMETHING

"Often when you think you are at the end of something, you're at the beginning of something else."

—FRED ROGERS

Tom and Sarah are now 62 years old, and they have significantly amplified their wealth. Their net worth is $15 million, and Tom has met the vesting requirements for his supplemental executive retirement plan. Tom's average annual salary and bonus over the past five years (excluding long-term incentive awards) has been approximately $1 million.

Tom could retire from Silica-Corp tomorrow with a monthly pension (qualified and SERP) of $42,000. His portfolio could generate an additional $25,000 per month of lifetime withdrawals, using a conservative withdrawal rate of 2 percent annually.

For many, leaving the corporate world behind with an annual income of $800,000 ($67,000 per month) is the pinnacle of achievement—the ultimate American dream.

Tom faced a dilemma. Even though he "could" retire, he wondered if he "should" retire. Was he ready?

Tom has seen former colleagues retire who struggled. Not financially per se but emotionally. They tied their identity and self-worth to their careers and job titles. For the last several years, he has been "Tom, Executive Vice President of Manufacturing for Silica-Corp." How would he feel once he retires and becomes just "Tom"? Tom was nervous that he might struggle in this next phase of life.

Tom's concerns are shared by many Section 16 officers considering retirement. Although stressful at times, the work environment provides structure to the day. Tom's work offers an opportunity for socialization with coworkers and a sense of purpose in working toward the company's common goals. How will that be replaced in retirement?

Tom's anxiety surrounding retirement comes from the unknown. We fear what we cannot foresee. In a previous chapter, we talked about temporal myopia. Tom is having difficulty seeing himself in the future as "retired." Tom needs to shift his mindset from *retiring from* Silica-Corp to *retiring to* something else.

That "something else" does not have to be another job or second career. Some retirees might be excited about a new career path, but for many, they will define retirement by the hobbies they want to pursue, the travel they want to accomplish, or volunteer work they would like to perform. By brainstorming ideas for how he will spend his time, Tom and Sarah can bring some structure to the concept of "retirement," which will help reduce their temporal myopia and fear of the unknown.

Ask yourself these questions as you contemplate retirement:

- If money were not a consideration, how would I spend my days?
- What motivates me in life?
- Am I "sick of working" or just "sick of working for my current employer"?
- Do I have an interest in working part time or starting my own business?
- Will my family support my decision?

The last question is essential. Will your family support your decision to retire?

Television host David Letterman retired in 2015 from *The Late Show*. He was 68 years old and said he wanted to "spend more time with his family." Two years later, he was done with retirement and announced he was bringing a new interview show to Netflix. When asked for thoughts on retirement, Letterman said:

> Here's what I have learned. If you retire to spend more time with your family, check with your family first.

I am sure part of Letterman's wisecrack was for comedic purposes, but it exposes a common issue. The spouse of a new retiree (and any children living at home) has their own schedule, motivations, and desires. In Tom's case, he spent decades following a particular routine with Silica-Corp. If Tom were suddenly home twenty-four hours a day, natural disruptions to his spouse and children's schedules would occur.

Establishing an active schedule benefits both the retiree and their family. Three endeavors where Section 16 retirees have found success are:

- Serving on corporate boards of directors
- Volunteering
- Entrepreneurship—starting their own business

CORPORATE BOARDS

For Section 16 officers, one of the most rewarding and lucrative part-time positions in retirement is serving on one or more corporate boards.

The board is responsible for the company's mission, vision, and values and for making sure the company's actions and policies adhere to that mission. Directors who serve on a corporate board are responsible for the oversight and governance of the company.

Board members have often been leaders in their field, and many have held Section 16 positions in the past. They bring unique expertise and experience to the board and valuable contacts within the industry.

The time commitment of board members can be significant. Board members will attend up to six to eight meetings per year in person, plus the travel time to and from those meetings must be considered. Board members will also participate in a handful of conference calls/web meetings between face-to-face discussions and serve on at least one committee under the board of directors. Board members also need to be "on-call" whenever unexpected issues or emergencies arise. For smaller companies, board members might be called on weekly for guidance and mentorship to assist companies through various growth stages.

Even though the time commitment for board members can be significant, so too are the financial rewards.

Compensation for board members typically includes the following:

- Annual retainer
- Stipend per meeting
- Reimbursement for travel costs to meetings
- Stock-based compensation

For private companies, which tend to be smaller, the annual retainer might be modest, in the $5,000–$10,000 range, with total compensation in the $20,000–$25,000 range. The stock-based compensation might be worthless in the early years. However, if the company has a liquidity event such as an IPO, stock-based compensation might soar. Imagine if you were one of the early board members of Apple or Amazon before they went public.

For publicly traded companies, compensation for board members is significantly higher.

In a 2018 survey of 300 publicly traded companies, compensation consulting firm FW Cook reported that small-cap companies paid their board members an average of $152,000. For mid-cap companies, the average board member received $205,000 of compensation. For large-cap companies, board member compensation jumped to $275,000.

Not all board positions are as lucrative. Warren Buffett's Berkshire Hathaway corporation pays their directors $900 for each meeting attended in person and $300 for each session joined via phone. Microsoft co-founder Bill Gates is a Berkshire Hathaway board member and received $3,300 for his services in 2018. Berkshire Hathaway does not provide any stock-based compensation to directors.

SEEKING BOARD POSITIONS

Experience: If you have never served on a board before, consider improving your résumé by serving on a nonprofit organization's board to develop skills and experience valued by a for-profit board. Aspire to serve on the finance committee of the nonprofit, where you would have fiduciary responsibility for financial matters.

Promotion: Promote your accomplishments and the value you have created in previous positions. Consider publishing articles in your field of expertise and speaking at industry conferences.

Networking: Many board members find their positions through their existing network. Let your network know you are interested in board opportunities. Reach out to people who are already on the board of a company you wish to target. Consider attending events sponsored by the National Association of Corporate Directors, an educational organization with over 21,000 active directors as members.

EXECUTIVE VOLUNTEER POSITIONS

When people think of volunteering in retirement, they might imagine serving food at a local soup kitchen or swinging a hammer to build a Habitat for Humanity home. Those positions are popular ways to give back to communities, but there are additional volunteer opportunities available for retired executives.

Charities need the same strategic planning, marketing, finance, and managerial assistance as for-profit organizations. It can be challenging for nonprofits to hire executive talent for these positions because they must compete with pay packages offered in the for-profit world. Retired Section 16 officers can use their knowledge, skills, and executive experience to immediately impact many nonprofit organizations as a volunteer.

A retired chief financial officer could work with the charity's accounting department. A former chief marketing officer could assist with advertising campaigns for new donors. A retiree from a corporate legal department could review contracts or negotiate leases.

Sometimes retirees think they are "too old" to be attractive to a charity, but with age comes experience. Formal education can give anyone *knowledge* regardless of age, but sometimes you need real-world experience to turn knowledge into *wisdom*.

"Knowledge is knowing that a tomato is a fruit. Wisdom is knowing not to put it in a fruit salad."

—BRIAN O'DRISCOLL

When discussing volunteer positions with clients who think

they are too old, I tell the story of "Hank" (not his real name), a retired CEO volunteering in a remote area of Africa. Hank was part of an international volunteer organization building an irrigation system to bring water to a small village. Water was a scarce commodity in this part of Africa, with the village women typically walking four miles each day to get water back to the community.

Hank was a "worker bee" on this trip, digging ditches and installing pipes for the water system. He was working alongside younger volunteers, many of whom had just graduated from college. His fellow volunteers did not know his previous work experience. Hank was just another volunteer who reminded the younger workers of their grandfather.

After months of progress on the irrigation system, the leader of this volunteer project, Simon, approached the crew with some bad news. A local tribal/political leader, the "mayor" of a neighboring village, rescinded a previous right-of-way agreement allowing pipes to pass through their land. The project came to a halt. Simon met with the mayor, who said the construction work would be too disruptive to his village, and his village already had access to water. The mayor ordered the volunteer crew to find a new route for the irrigation system away from their land. There was no appeal. His decision was final.

Simon was an exceptional team leader, knowledgeable in the water system's construction requirements. He first came to Africa two years earlier as a new college graduate, and he worked on a different irrigation system. After completing his first water project, the charity promoted Simon to "team leader" for the new project. Simon had all the *knowledge* required to build the irrigation system but did not yet have the *wisdom* that can only come from experience. Simon had never encountered someone like this mayor.

Simon told the crew to stop all work. They would need to install an additional three miles of pipe to reroute around the village. Simon needed to get the appropriate approvals from his superiors in the United States before proceeding.

Hank asked Simon how long that could take, and Simon said it could be two weeks or two months. For now, all they could do was wait.

Hank asked if he could meet the mayor. Simon did not think that would be possible or even allowed since Simon was the team leader and Hank had not gone through the "team leader training" before coming to Africa. Hank persisted, and he told Simon a bit about his background. Hank was modest, but he impressed upon Simon that he had spent his entire career negotiating with clients, vendors, and political representatives. After all, what did they have to lose? They would otherwise be sitting around for two weeks or two months. Why not invest in one more conversation?

Simon agreed to let Hank speak with the mayor and scheduled the meeting for the next day.

The mayor told Hank the same thing he told Simon, that construction would be too disruptive to the village. This village already had a water system, so it was not benefiting his people. It was only disrupting their day-to-day routine while construction went through their land.

Hank asked more probing questions. He wanted to learn about the disruptions concerning the mayor. Hank found out during the meeting that the primary anxiety was with the cattle ranchers who move their cattle from the pens to the fields every day to feed. Once the trenching starts for the waterway, the ranchers will need to move the cattle through a hilly section of the village to bypass the construction and make it to the fields.

Hank asked the mayor, "So if we bypassed your village completely, there would be no impact on the day-to-day routine of the cattle herd, correct?" The mayor said that is what he was trying to accomplish.

Hank asked, "What if we built a footbridge over the construction area, allowing the cattle to safely traverse the trenches without needing to navigate the hilly section of the village?"

The mayor said that would be helpful, but he did not want to set a precedent for future construction projects. If he said yes to this plan, it might be hard to say no to the next organization that needed assistance.

"What if we built a *removable* footbridge, so that once we finish this project, if another request comes along, you will already be prepared to assist with no need to reroute the cattle?"

The mayor agreed.

It took the crew six days and $2,500 worth of lumber to build the bridge, but it saved weeks (or months) of uncertainty waiting for the charity's US office to approve the reroute of the project. For a $2,500 investment, Hank potentially saved tens of thousands of dollars of additional cost if they had to move the water project three miles around the village.

Although Hank went to Africa to dig ditches, he found that his negotiating skills as a former CEO were invaluable to the project. Hank had something the younger volunteers did not— wisdom that came from experience. Age is just a number.

WHERE TO FIND EXECUTIVE VOLUNTEER POSITIONS

Executive Service Corp—US: https://www.escus.org/volunteer/

Taproot Foundation: https://taprootfoundation.org/

Score: https://www.score.org/volunteer

Financial Services Volunteer Corps: https://www.fsvc.org/

For a more complete list of resources and current web links, please visit our website at: www.Section16Secrets.com

ENTREPRENEURSHIP

Age *is* just a number. When people think of entrepreneurs, they think of Mark Zuckerberg or Steve Jobs developing their companies from a dorm room or garage and that it's a young person's game.

Not necessarily.

Duke University researchers surveyed 652 tech-company founders, generating at least $1 million of revenue, who started companies between 1995 and 2005. They found that nearly five times as many founders were over the age of 45 when they started their companies, compared to founders younger than 25.[1]

Retired Section 16 officers may have a better chance of becoming successful entrepreneurs when compared to younger business owners because:

- They are typically in a better financial position to start a company.
- They have more contacts and professional relationships in the business world.
- Their children are grown, and their personal lives are more stable.
- They understand what their weaknesses are. When you are 60 years old, you have a good idea of your skills *and* weaknesses. If you ask the average 25-year-old what their weaknesses are, many will tell you they have none.

There are different levels, or ranges, of entrepreneurship.

Not every successful auto mechanic wants to build the next Midas Muffler corporation, and not every chef wants to create a chain to compete with 900 Olive Garden locations. Many professionals are well-suited to become self-employed and earn an excellent living, even if the endgame is not to build a company with 1,000 employees.

For retired Section 16 officers, their skills can be in high demand as consultants. If they no longer want to "manage people," they can be a one-person show—what we call solo entrepreneurs or solopreneurs.

You might be passionate about building a consulting career where you can work as much or as little as you want, be responsible for your time, and perhaps hire an assistant to manage your scheduling and administrative tasks. Your post-retirement consulting career can be rewarding, both professionally and financially, even if the endgame is not to hire one hundred junior consultants and grow into the next McKinsey & Company.

AND NOW FOR SOMETHING COMPLETELY DIFFERENT

Sometimes retired Section 16 officers look for business ventures that are entirely outside of their professional skillset. When you have spent your entire career managing people, perhaps the last thing you want to do is start a venture with numerous direct reports. If you have lived half of your corporate life in airports or other countries, you may desire a business that requires zero travel.

My friend and client Fritz (not his real name) recently retired from his Section 16 position with a Fortune 100 company in the Midwest. He traveled the world for this company and even lived in South Korea for a few years while his wife, Linda, remained in the United States.

Shortly before retirement, he purchased a home in Oregon's farm country outside Portland. The house had some apple trees and some land that a local farmer leased for growing crops. Recently, another parcel of land became available, currently used for farming blueberries, marionberries, and other crops. Fritz and Linda purchased this land as an investment property, not interested in the farming potential at the time but rather for some potential development use down the road.

As Fritz settled into retirement, he started working more on his land. Fritz took over some work previously done by tenant farmers. One day, Linda sent me a photo of Fritz on a small John Deere tractor working in the field.

My wife and I had a chance to visit with Fritz and Linda in Oregon in 2020 and take a tour of their land. What started as a small "hobby" was now 200 acres producing apples, blueberries, marionberries, strawberries, and other crops. Fritz opened up one of their barns and showed us the equipment he had accumulated over the past few years. The small John Deere tractor was still there, but so were tractors with tires taller than me, a large combine machine, and many other implements.

My wife was not familiar with Fritz's corporate history, other than knowing he recently retired.

"So how long have you been farming?" she asked him and was surprised at his answer.

"Just a couple of years."

She later told me she assumed all along that Fritz had been farming in addition to his work in the corporate world. She was amazed that all his knowledge of the farming industry had come in just a short time.

Fritz and Linda found a venture they are passionate about, and they might never have more than a handful of employees. I know that Fritz has the managerial skills to grow his "family farm" of 200 acres into a corporate giant of 20,000 acres if that was his goal, but it is not. "Farmer Fritz" is living the retirement dream. In some ways, he is now busier than he was in the corporate world. Fritz shared that with his Section 16 position, he felt like his "hair was on fire all of the time." With the farm, it is a different set of fires, and it forces him to learn something new every day, which keeps him healthy both physically and mentally.

Tom and Sarah started to get excited about the prospects of retirement. The idea of volunteering in Africa like Hank was very appealing, and it is something they could do together. Sarah always had an interest in horticulture, so perhaps they could move in the direction of Fritz and Linda and add a greenhouse to their property and start a flower business. Sarah could handle the gardening, and Tom could run the business details.

For the first time in our retirement discussion, Tom and Sarah were now looking at retiring "to" something, and not just retiring "from" Silica-Corp. As their excitement for this next chapter in their lives increased, their temporal myopia started to fade, and they could see their future more clearly.

When you get excited for "what comes next," you want that part of your life to be long and fulfilling. In our next chapter, we will review longevity in retirement and ways to improve and increase our remaining time in this world.

CHAPTER 12

LONGEVITY IN RETIREMENT

WHAT IS YOUR BIOLOGICAL AGE?

"My parents didn't want to move to Florida, but they turned sixty, and that's the law."

—JERRY SEINFELD

For older generations, retirement meant working until age 65, until they could collect Social Security and then kick back and relax. Many might live only five to ten years in retirement. There was not much need for long-term retirement planning in the past.

Retirement is different for younger generations. Workers are retiring earlier and living longer. It is not uncommon for some retirees to have twenty-five years or more ahead of them. That is a long time to "kick back and relax."

It is essential for modern retirees to remain active, both physically and mentally, and build a retirement life that will motivate and challenge them for years to come.

Retirement is not the end of the game; it's just the beginning of the second half.

The *Journal of Gerontology* published their first issue in 1946 with the slogan of:

To add life to years, not just years to life.

Living longer is an admirable goal, but there should be a well-defined reason behind the desire. Longevity alone may not be an enjoyable experience. Do you want to live longer because you are "having a great time," or do you want to live longer because of a fear of the unknown or a fear of death?

What if you were 95 and living in a nursing home? Your mobility is gone, you see visitors only on the weekend, and you do not have the capacity for deep and meaningful conversations. Would you be looking forward to your 100th birthday?

Instead, what if you were 95, and you were traveling to your winter home this month? Not so much to get away from the cold but rather because you enjoy walking every day, and it is easier to do that outside with no snow. You need to be back up north by May at the latest because two of your great-grandchildren are graduating from high school, and you promised you would be there. You always prefer to attend meetings in person versus online, and one of the boards you volunteer on is having their annual meeting in June. One of your great-grandchildren is expecting their first child in September, and you would like to meet them face-to-face before heading south again for a few months. In the meantime, you must make sure you prep your winter home for your children, who will each be visiting for a week or two during the winter. Are you looking forward to your 100th birthday?

LOW-HANGING FRUIT

My mentor Dan Sullivan, who has coached thousands of entrepreneurs through his Strategic Coach® program, is fond of saying, "Death looks for the low-hanging fruit." If you are active, engaged, and having a good time, it is too hard for the grim reaper to focus on you right now. Death will wait for a better opportunity.

I see this with some of our clients. I work with people in their 80s (and even 90s) who still golf weekly. Some attend aerobics or swimming classes each week, too. A client in her 80s traveled across the country to see Adele in concert with her friends. Some other clients in their 80s regularly travel out of state to see their grandchildren in school plays. Another client became a published author at close to 80—what an accomplishment. Does death want to waste time on these active people right now? They are too hard to catch!

Compare those active and engaged octogenarians to others you might know—people who seem to be "ready to die," regardless of their age. They have strained relationships with their children or grandchildren, and perhaps they do not see them often. They have too many "aches and pains" to walk around the neighborhood anymore. Whenever they run into friends or acquaintances, they load up their conversation with complaints about anything—their health, children, neighbors, or politics. You name it. They do not have an interest in learning anything new to keep their mind active, because after all, you "can't teach an old dog new tricks." Relative to the vibrant and engaging 80-year-olds mentioned in the previous paragraph, these people seem to be the "low-hanging fruit" just waiting to move on.

Having a mindset of positivity will assist with longevity, but it is not the only thing—especially for Section 16 officers and other executives.

Many of these professionals sacrifice their health during their careers. They do not exercise enough (or at all), and their eating habits are poor because they are always traveling. The list goes on. In addition to the correct mindset for longevity, executives must help the process by improving their health habits today.

HEALTHSPAN VERSUS LIFESPAN

Improving longevity is a worthy goal for most, but what if you lived to age 90 or 100 and you were chronically ill, lost your mobility, or lost your mental acuity? Would you still want to live that long?

When we think of age, we tend to think in chronological numbers, which is lifespan—the number of years someone has been alive. In the United States, the average lifespan is approximately 79 years.

My goal is to live to age 105. I would like to attend the 50th high school anniversary jubilee celebration for my youngest son in 2073, when I am 104 years old (and he will be 68!). The year 2073 also corresponds with my eightieth wedding anniversary. I am looking forward to some pretty cool milestones in 2073.

I am not interested in increasing my *lifespan* to 105 unless my *healthspan* can follow. Healthspan reflects your quality of life—the number of healthy and functional years. Just because the average life expectancy is 79 in the United States does not mean everyone lives those 79 years healthy and functional.

The World Health Organization (WHO) has researched what they call Healthy Life Expectancy (HALE). According to their most recent data, the average healthy life expectancy in the United States is approximately 68 ½ years. If the average life expectancy is 79, that means the average US citizen is living for more than a decade with some form of health issue—13 percent of their life.

Your chronological age is a clear indicator of your lifespan thus far, and everyone can calculate their chronological age. We tend to celebrate that calculation annually on our birthday.

The age that will most influence our healthspan is our biological age. Biological age refers to how old a person seems or feels.

We have all been in situations where we have met someone and we could not believe how young (or old) they appeared, relative to their chronological age. I have met people at the gym who have asked me to "guess their age." Some of those people are 80 years old (their chronological age), but they could easily pass for someone 65 (perhaps closer to their biological age).

It is not as easy to measure biological age. There is no standard-ized measurement like there is for chronological age. Biological age considers many lifestyle factors, such as diet, exercise, sleep-ing habits, stress levels, quality of personal relationships, and so forth.

CARDIORESPIRATORY FITNESS AND VO₂ MAX

Your *VO₂ Max score* is a good predictor of biological age.

VO_2 Max is the maximum rate of oxygen consumption during exercise/activity of increasing intensity. The name comes from the abbreviations of volume (V), oxygen (O_2), and maximum (Max). VO_2 Max is considered the best indicator of *cardiore-spiratory fitness.*

Most people are familiar with *cardiovascular fitness and endur-ance,* which is your heart and blood vessels' ability to transport blood during exertion or exercise. As your workout intensity increases, your muscles need more fuel as they produce addi-tional waste. This need for energy causes your heart rate to increase, which puts more stress on your vascular system of arteries, veins, and capillaries. Increased cardiovascular fitness is associated with improved heart health and reduced instances of heart disease.

Cardiorespiratory fitness measures not only your heart and vas-cular system but your lungs as well. The vascular system carries oxygen-rich blood from your lungs to your muscles, and part of the waste carried away by the vascular system is carbon dioxide, exhaled by the lungs. Cardiorespiratory fitness is your heart, lungs, and muscles' ability to work *together* for extended periods.

A person's VO_2 Max score typically declines with chronological age. A 60-year-old should have a lower VO_2 Max score than a 40-year-old. Notice that I said "should" have a lower VO_2 Max score. A 60-year-old with a consistent regiment of cardiorespiratory exercise may have a higher VO_2 Max score than a sedentary 40-year-old.

VO_2 Max can be a good indicator of biological age and predictor of longevity. By comparing your VO_2 Max score to the average VO_2 Max scores for people younger, older, and the same age as you, you can get an idea of your biological age. If you are 60 years old and your VO_2 Max score is the same as a typical 40-year-old, your biological age might be twenty years younger than what your driver's license says.

Although having a VO_2 Max score of someone twenty years younger than you can boost your self-esteem, studies have shown it can also increase your lifespan. The American Heart Association has found that low levels of cardiorespiratory fitness (low VO_2 Max) are associated with a higher risk of cardiovascular disease, higher all-cause mortality, and higher mortality rates attributable to certain cancers. They also state that a growing body of clinical evidence demonstrates that cardiorespiratory fitness is potentially a more robust predictor of mortality than established risk factors such as smoking, hypertension, high cholesterol, and type 2 diabetes.

HOW DO YOU IMPROVE YOUR VO_2 MAX AND CARDIORESPIRATORY FITNESS?

Regular exercise is important, but anything that is "regular" or becomes regular over time will simply allow you to maintain, not improve, your fitness level. If you are walking two miles around your neighborhood every morning, and every morning it takes you exactly thirty minutes to finish that route, then you are not "improving." You are "maintaining."

Technology has made it easier to track our fitness. Smartphones and wearable devices, such as the Fitbit® and Apple Watch have brought daily "step counts" into our vocabulary. Goals such as walking 10,000 steps per day have become increasingly popular, in part because they are easy to understand.

Walking more, parking a bit farther away in your office parking lot, and taking the stairs instead of the elevator are all good ideas. You will maintain (or slightly improve) your health, and you will see motivational rewards pop up on your Fitbit tracker.

If you want to improve your cardiorespiratory fitness, step counts leave out a critical component, which is intensity. Someone who walks 10,000 steps over an entire day puts in a different level of effort than someone who runs 10,000 steps over an hour.

Low-intensity activities such as walking do not typically engage your cardiorespiratory system. It is not challenging enough. High-intensity activities, such as jogging/running, hiking up inclines (or using a StairMaster), cycling, rowing, and swimming engage your cardiorespiratory system, even over short periods. The benefit from even short bursts of all-out effort has given rise to the popular training method known as high-intensity interval training (HIIT).

HIIT inserts short bursts of high-intensity activity in between more moderate activities. For example, you might jog (or even walk) at an average pace for two minutes, followed by a high-intensity sprint for thirty seconds, and then go back to a normal walking or jogging pace for another two minutes and repeat. The goal is to put forth your maximum effort during that thirty-second period, to really increase your heart rate, and then rest and repeat.

When you challenge your cardiorespiratory system frequently with increasing intensity, it starts to adapt to prepare itself for the next challenge. This adaptation results in a higher VO_2 Max score. As your VO_2 Max score continues to improve, you will need to adjust your workouts to increase your intensity further. An exercise that might have challenged you two months ago might not generate the same physiological response today.

HOW TO MEASURE YOUR VO_2 MAX

Now that you have committed to improving your cardiorespiratory fitness, how do you measure your success? A saying most Section 16 officers are familiar with is "What gets measured gets done."

Although some fitness trackers can approximate your VO_2 Max score, the most accurate reading will come from specialized equipment in a laboratory setting, a holistic health center, or some performance gyms.

To measure your VO_2 Max, you will wear a mask and a heart rate monitor while exercising on either a treadmill or stationary bicycle. The mask connects to a machine that will measure and record the amount of oxygen you inhale and the amount of air and carbon dioxide you exhale. Your workout's intensity on the treadmill or bike will increase throughout the test. The technician or physician monitoring the test will increase the treadmill's speed or the bicycle's resistance until your oxygen consumption remains steady throughout the increase in intensity.

Once your oxygen consumption plateaus and you have reached your "maximum" consumption despite an increase in intensity, your body will move from an aerobic state to an anaerobic state—your body stops using oxygen as fuel in an anaerobic state because there is not enough oxygen to consume. This is your VO_2 Max, and once you hit it, your workout's intensity also plateaus, and your muscles start to fatigue. You must reduce the intensity and return to an aerobic state to keep going.

If you cannot test your VO_2 Max in a professional setting, you can arrive at an approximate number using two heart rate measurements: your maximum heart rate and your resting heart rate.

The calculation is VO_2 Max = 15.3 × MHR/RHR

Once you have your VO_2 Max score, you can compare yourself to the average numbers in the table below (table from *Men's Running* magazine):

WOMEN							
Age	Very Poor	Poor	Fair	Average	Good	Very Good	Excellent
20-24	<27	27-31	32-36	37-41	42-46	47-51	>51
25-29	<26	26-30	31-35	36-40	41-44	45-49	>49
30-34	<25	25-29	30-33	34-37	38-42	43-46	>46
35-39	<24	24-27	28-31	32-35	36-40	41-44	>44
40-44	<22	22-25	26-29	30-33	34-37	38-41	>41
45-49	<21	21-23	24-27	28-31	32-35	36-38	>38
50-54	<19	19-22	23-25	26-29	30-32	33-36	>36
55-59	<18	18-20	21-23	24-27	28-30	31-33	>33
60-65	<16	16-18	19-21	22-24	25-27	28-30	>30

MEN							
Age	Very Poor	Poor	Fair	Average	Good	Very Good	Excellent
20-24	<32	32-37	38-43	44-50	51-56	57-62	>62
25-29	<31	31-35	36-42	43-48	49-53	54-59	>59
30-34	<29	29-34	35-40	41-45	46-51	52-56	>56
35-39	<28	28-32	33-38	39-43	44-48	49-54	>54
40-44	<26	26-31	32-35	36-41	42-46	47-51	>51
45-49	<25	25-29	30-34	35-39	40-43	44-48	>48
50-54	<24	24-27	28-32	33-36	37-41	42-46	>46
55-59	<22	22-26	27-30	31-34	35-39	40-43	>43
60-65	<21	21-24	25-28	29-32	33-36	37-40	>40

If you are a 55-year-old male, a VO₂ Max score of forty-five puts you in the "excellent" category for your age. If you could increase your VO₂ Max score to fifty-five, you would be in the excellent category for a 35-year-old.

The key is not your specific score today but rather the trend. Once you establish your baseline, you can track your improvement over time. When you think of VO_2 Max in terms of your biological age, maintaining the same score while your chronological age increases is like "freezing time." If you can improve your VO_2 Max score even as your chronological age moves higher, then you might be "turning back the clock."

RESISTANCE TRAINING AND LONGEVITY

Expanding your cardiorespiratory fitness will improve your biological age. Still, studies have shown that resistance training, also called strength training or weightlifting, is equally important if your goal is to improve your healthspan and not just your lifespan.

Section 16 executives are especially prone to losing muscle mass as they age. Since "time is money," assistants make sure that executive schedules are ultra-efficient, sometimes removing natural movements that can build strength and endurance. They schedule meetings in offices close to each other, so there is no time wasted walking between buildings. If an appointment is offsite, a car will pick up the executive to drive them to an engagement even a few blocks away. Air travel is usually on the company plane, and a driver brings the officer to the executive terminal near the tarmac. There is no fast-paced walking through the airport carrying luggage. A meeting on the tenth floor of a building means the executive has a few minutes in the elevator to check email on their phone—that time will not be "wasted" taking the stairs.

"Humans evolved as a species that walks, runs, climbs trees and hills, and uses a variety of muscles all the time. Now people use elevators and escalators instead of stairs, drive instead of walk,

use dishwashers and washing machines instead of washing dishes and clothes by hand, buy food instead of growing it, and hire people to do even minor repair work around the house instead of fixing things ourselves."

—DR. VALTER LONGO

SARCOPENIA (MUSCLE LOSS DUE TO AGING)

Sarcopenia originates from Greek and translates as "lack of flesh." As we age, our muscle mass declines. The average person will lose about a quarter of their age-30 muscle strength by 70, and half of it by 90. "Just doing aerobic exercise is not adequate," says Dr. Robert Schreiber, an instructor in medicine at Harvard Medical School. "Unless you are doing strength training, you will become weaker and less functional."[2]

Maintaining functionality as we age is the key to longevity. You want to be able to walk up the steps to your home, load groceries into the car, and lift your grandchildren. Do you remember the Tin Man from the *Wizard of Oz*? Just like the Tin Man, if we stand still for too long, we will "rust up" until we can ultimately no longer move at all.

Regular strength training not only improves muscle mass and functionality but also improves bone density. Increased strength, especially leg strength, means you are less likely to stumble and fall as you age. Increased bone density means you will hopefully not suffer any broken bones if you do fall.

Most of us have an elderly friend or relative who was "doing so well" until they fell and broke their hip. Now they are in a nursing home. Perhaps you know someone who broke their leg and was in a wheelchair during their rehabilitation phase, but even after their leg healed, they remained in the wheelchair. Lack of strength leads to a loss of function, which increases the chances of falls, which increases the chances of broken bones, which ultimately reduces our mobility. Once our mobility is gone, a reduction in healthspan *and* lifespan occurs.

Researchers from the Penn State College of Medicine examined data from the National Health Interview Survey collected between 1997 and 2001 and then compared it to death certificate data of more than 30,000 people through 2011. Only 9 percent of survey respondents reported strength training at least twice a week, but those individuals had a 46 percent less risk of early death than the other 91 percent with no strength training. These people were also 41 percent less likely to have a cardiac-related death and 19 percent less likely to die from cancer.[3]

GRIP STRENGTH AND LONGEVITY: A FIRM HANDSHAKE

We have all been on the receiving end of a weak handshake when the person's hand feels like a dead fish in our palms. As far as first impressions go, a firm handshake suggests poise and self-assurance, whereas people extending a weak handshake seem lacking in self-confidence.

What if your handshake could also be a predictor of longevity? Researchers have established a strong link between a person's grip strength and longevity. A 2018 study published in the *British Medical Journal* examined the grip strength of over 500,000 adults between the ages of 40 and 69 and compared the incidents of heart disease, respiratory disease, and cancers within this group. They found that lower grip strength measurements were associated with a higher overall mortality rate and risk of specific illnesses.

Some correlations from this study were astounding. Grip strength was shown to be a better predictor of future cardiovascular disease than traditional measurements such as blood pressure.[4]

A 2015 study published by *The Lancet* found similar results. This study examined almost 140,000 adults between age 35 and 70 from seventeen culturally and economically diverse countries. They found that every 5 kg decline in grip strength (measured with a handgrip dynamometer) was associated with a 17 percent increase in cardiovascular-related death.[5]

The relationship between grip strength and longevity does not seem intuitive, as perhaps the relationship between cardiovascular or cardiorespiratory health and longevity. Nonetheless, the relationship exists. Grip strength is one of those markers that can help reduce our biological age, making us feel, perform, and appear younger than we are.

Grip strength correlates highly with overall muscle mass, and we have already reviewed the importance of strength training for improved biological age and longevity. Grip strength also keeps us functional and functioning as we age. It improves or sustains our ability to carry groceries from the car to the kitchen, hold on to railings, and even open jars of pickles.

PLANNING TIP

You can purchase small handheld exercise devices to improve your grip strength. The cost is nominal, in the $15–$30 range. I keep a set of exercise tools in the car with me, so it is easy to get in a few squeezing repetitions at traffic lights during my commute.

THE MENTAL SIDE OF LONGEVITY: IT'S ALL IN YOUR HEAD

Physical activity, cardiorespiratory training, strength training, and grip strength are essential markers of longevity. Just as we train our bodies, it is also crucial to train our minds.

We all have had bad days. Perhaps your dog decided to run out the front door when you left for work, causing you to be late. Maybe you left your office late at night only to find that your car would not start. Most of us have experienced the embarrassment of sending an email to the wrong recipient because our email program "auto-filled" an incorrect email address.

What these mishaps have in common is that they tend to happen to all of us at some point. They also manage to work themselves out. The dog comes home, the car gets fixed, and the email gets rerouted correctly.

Some people take these short-term setbacks in stride. The bad stuff happens, and then they are over it. For others, they fixate on the bad stuff to the detriment of their health. Psychologists define the personality trait of someone who lives in a constant state of anxiety as neuroticism. Individuals with a high neuroticism score will appear "moody" to others. They tend to experience heightened worry, anxiety, fear, frustration, depression, and loneliness. Researchers at Purdue University have found that constant worrying and overreacting to life's curveballs can reduce life expectancy.[6]

Another theory on reduced life expectancy from heightened stress comes from high cortisol levels. Cortisol is the fight-or-flight hormone secreted when we are fearful or stressed out. Studies have shown that too much cortisol can negatively impact our immune system and heart health.

Our bodies are designed to protect us against threats from predators. Our early ancestors needed to avoid saber-toothed tigers; however, modern man has other threats. If you are walking across the street and see that a car ran a red light and is coming straight toward you, your body sets off an internal alarm and enters fight-or-flight mode, releasing a surge of cortisol and adrenaline. These hormones increase your heart rate, blood pressure, and energy supplies (by moving more sugars/glucose to your bloodstream).

Cortisol also reduces bodily functions deemed unnecessary to fight the threat at hand, such as your immune response and digestive system. If you need to run from a predator, your body puts all its energy and resources into escaping that threat. Your body no longer cares about digesting your last meal or sending immune-fighting cells to disable a cold virus.

The body's quick move into a fight-or-flight state is necessary to allow you to react immediately and get out of the path of that moving car (or saber-toothed tiger). The body's threat response is supposed to last only for the time of the perceived threat. Ten to thirty minutes after you have safely escaped the path of the moving car, your heart rate and blood pressure will start to return to normal, as your cortisol and adrenaline levels drop. As those hormones return to normal, the bodily functions that were temporarily disabled, such as your immune system, start to return to normal, too.

What if your body thinks it is in fight-or-flight mode when encountering "everyday" stressors, such as a project due at work, getting the kids to school, and paying the mortgage and other bills on time? When this occurs, cortisol levels remain constantly high, harming heart health through an increased heart rate and increased blood pressure.

Constant anxiety makes it easier for people to make unhealthy decisions—for example, excessive alcohol consumption or overeating. Have you heard of "comfort food"? Sometimes a tub of Ben & Jerry's ice cream is the only thing that will make someone feel better (in the short term). Cortisol influences appetite by binding to particular receptors in the brain, increasing cravings for high-calorie foods.

The body's reaction to chronic mental stress keeps us in a permanent state of fight-or-flight. For people who tend to live in a state of constant anxiety, finding ways to reduce stress can have a profound impact on their healthspan and longevity.

HOW CAN YOU BETTER MANAGE STRESS AND REDUCE CORTISOL LEVELS?

There are six components to managing stress and reducing cortisol levels: diet, sleep, exercise, meditation, drinking tea, and reducing inflammation.

DIET

Maintaining a healthy diet and reducing the amount of sugar you consume helps keep cortisol levels stable. It is also essential to drink plenty of water to keep cortisol levels in check.

SLEEP

Sleep impacts cortisol levels—and quantity and quality both matter. Try to go to bed and wake up on a consistent schedule daily. Get out of the habit of using your phone in bed, as the blue light emitted from electronic devices impacts your sleep cycle and circadian rhythms.

EXERCISE

Physical activity can also improve a person's mood. Strenuous exercise will trigger a short-term increase in cortisol levels, as your body reacts to the additional physical stress. That's okay because your body will start to learn that higher cortisol levels should be associated with physical stress and not necessarily an anxious mind.

MEDITATION

Meditation is one of the best ways to help "calm your mind." Even five minutes a day of meditation and focused breathing can improve your ability to relax and reduce cortisol levels. Many apps are available for digital devices and smartphones to help you get started, such as *Insight Timer*, *Calm*, and *Breathe*.

DRINK TEA

Green tea contains an amino acid L-theanine, shown to reduce stress and cortisol levels. If you are not a tea drinker, you can take an over-the-counter L-theanine supplement. Of course, before taking any supplements, please make sure to consult with your physician.

REDUCE INFLAMMATION

Inflammation is the body's response to an invading or foreign threat, such as a cold virus, cancer, or an emotional or psychological stressor. When we are inflamed, the immune system dispatches various chemicals (pro-inflammatory cytokines) to attack the threat. These pro-inflammatory cytokines are supposed to do their job (eliminate the threat) and then disappear. If your body is in a state of chronic inflammation (due to constant anxiety or stress), however, these pro-inflammatory cytokines remain upregulated. One of the best ways to reduce chronic inflammation is by increasing the amount of omega-3 fatty acids you consume. You could accomplish this by eating certain types of fish a few times per week, such as salmon or mackerel. Alternatively, you can utilize fish oil supplements. Of course, before taking any supplements, please make sure to consult with your physician.

INFLAMMATION TEST

The ratio of omega-6 to omega-3 fatty acids in our ancestors' diets was approximately one-to-one. Today, as Western cultures have become addicted to vegetable oils and processed foods, that ratio is estimated to be between ten- and twenty-to-one. Some researchers believe the increase of omega-6 fats and the decrease of omega-3 fats in the standard American diet is associated with the rise in chronic inflammatory diseases.[7] What is the acronym for the standard American diet? SAD!

Dr. Barry Sears from ZoneLabs offers a quick cellular inflammation blood test. A simple finger-prick of blood will measure your cellular inflammation by the ratio of omega-6 fats to omega-3 fats. Dr. Sears believes that elevated cellular inflammation levels are the underlying cause of many chronic diseases and why some people seem to age faster.

Visit http://www.zonediet.com/ for additional information about their test.

HEART RATE VARIABILITY AND LONGEVITY

Heart rate variability (HRV) is the variance in time between the beats of your heart. For example, if your heart rate is sixty beats per minute, it is not beating exactly one beat every second. Your first beat might be at one second, your second beat at 1.9 seconds, your third beat at 3.1 seconds, and so on. The greater the variability between beats, the more prepared your body is to take on strain and execute at a high level.

Although HRV is a cardiovascular measurement, it is a marker of your autonomic nervous system. HRV helps us understand the balance between your nervous system's sympathetic and parasympathetic branches. Your autonomic nervous system controls your involuntary bodily functions (such as heartbeats, blood pressure, breathing, digestion, etc.).

You need a quick response for short-term survival (e.g., outrunning predators). The sympathetic nervous system (SNS) is referred to as the "fight-or-flight" side, allowing you to react to threats quickly. The parasympathetic nervous system (PNS) is the "rest and digest" or relaxation side, needed for *long-term* survival.

What happens if you are always in "fight-or-flight" mode due to chronic stress? Your body might have an inability to turn on the parasympathetic side of your nervous system, so you are rarely in a rest-and-digest state.

Someone with a low HRV score will have either an upregulated sympathetic response or suppressed parasympathetic activity. A low HRV score indicates that your body cannot enter recovery mode. A low HRV could be a temporary response to poor dietary choices the day before (e.g., ingesting a lot of sugar), or perhaps you had an intense workout. It could also be caused by chronic stress in your life, resulting in reduced healthspan and lifespan.

Someone with low heart rate variability is at an increased risk of disease, inflammation, anxiety, and a reduced fitness level. All of these items can increase your biological age.

So how can you increase your HRV? All the strategies for reducing stress and cortisol levels apply to *increasing* your HRV. Improve your diet, sleep, exercise, meditation practices, and reduce cellular inflammation.

HOW CAN YOU MEASURE YOUR HEART RATE VARIABILITY?

The best way to measure HRV is to analyze the per-beat results from an electrocardiogram—the test you have done in a medical office with the wires attached to your chest. Although accurate, this is not very practical for ongoing training and analysis.

Several companies have developed apps and monitors allowing you to measure your HRV at home. Some monitors will connect to a chest strap and some to a wearable device such as a wristband or ring. HRV monitors are not regulated medical devices, so the accuracy across different types of monitors or manufacturers will vary. The number on any one day is not as important as your trend. HRV can provide general insight into the flexibility of your autonomic nervous system and your brain's ability to switch back and forth between fight-or-flight and relaxation modes.

HRV MEASUREMENT

I utilize the Whoop™ wrist strap to track my HRV and other performance metrics. Each morning Whoop provides me a measurement of my HRV from the night before, making it easy to spot trends over time. I will offer a deeper dive into Whoop in the next chapter.

FASTING AND LONGEVITY

Doctors, nutritionists, personal trainers, and the media place a lot of emphasis on our diets. Most of us know that eating well is one of the pillars of good health. What if I told you that "when" we eat can be just as important as "what" we eat.

Fasting is when you restrict your calorie intake for a certain period. You could limit your eating to certain times of the day or even certain days of the week.

There have been many studies about the benefits of fasting. Fasting has become a buzzword in the nutrition world over the past few years. A Google search of "intermittent fasting" returns almost 18 million results.

Fasting is not new. It was a part of everyday life for early humans. When we were hunter-gatherers, we would have a big meal when food was killed or collected, and then we would fast until food became available again. Our ancestors also followed a natural circadian rhythm—eating during daylight hours when food was available and fasting overnight until they could look for food again the next day.

Life is much easier for modern man, but easier is not always better. Easy refrigeration, food processing, and access to light twenty-four hours a day have changed our eating habits. We have many food options available to us, and artificial light has extended our eating window indefinitely. We live in a world where many humans in Western cultures have access to food every minute of the day, and the food is not always *good*. Our bodies were not made to eat around the clock.

Fasting depletes our cells of nutrients, which kills off weak or damaged cells. Our next meal will replenish our robust and healthy cells. When we are constantly eating, our bodies never get a break to restore and replenish our healthy cells.

Studies have shown a promising connection between fasting and longevity and overall metabolic health. In one study, mice who only ate one meal per day lived approximately 11 percent longer than mice who had access to food at any time during the day. These mice lived longer even though they ate roughly the same total amount of food. The fasting group also developed fewer diseases as they aged, compared to the mice who could eat whenever they wanted.[8]

Dr. Valter Longo at the University of Southern California tested a fasting diet with mice. The control group was given a restricted diet for four days, then their regular diet for ten days, and then repeated. So two times a month, the mice were on the calorie-restricted diet, and this went on for several months. At the end of the study, the calorie-restricted mice had lower blood sugar and insulin levels, greater bone density, less visceral fat around their organs, and increased nerve cell development in their brains.[9]

Dr. Longo then conducted a human study with a small group. Nineteen healthy adults consumed a plant-based diet that provided between 34 percent and 54 percent of a regular caloric intake over five days. This five-day diet was repeated once a month for three months, so participants were calorie-restricted for fifteen out of ninety days.

Compared to a control group of another nineteen healthy adults, the participants on the five-day restricted diet had improvements in their blood glucose levels and a decrease in body weight. Those participants with initially elevated C-reactive protein levels (one of the markers of heart disease risk) had lower levels at the end of the study, and those with normal levels had no change.[10]

FASTING PLANS

There are multiple types of fasting plans you can consider. Two of the more popular choices are *intermittent fasting (IF)* and *water fasts.*

Also known as time-restricted eating, IF has become "trendy" over the past few years. It is a pattern that cycles between periods of eating and periods of *not* eating (fasting). Instead of intermittent *fasting*, the process could also be called intermittent *eating.* You can cycle through these periods of eating (or not eating) daily or over several days.

The most common intermittent fasting plan is the 16/8 method. You are eating in an eight-hour window and fasting for the remaining sixteen hours of the day. Your first meal of the day might occur at noon, with your last meal finishing by 8:00 p.m. You are then fasting from 8:00 p.m. through noon the following day.

Water fasting is as the name implies. You consume only water for a certain period, typically three to five days. This fasting method is more extreme, so you should not attempt it every week. Some people will water fast once per month for a few months and then once per quarter on a long-term basis.

The metabolic benefits of three- to five-day fasting are more significant than the shorter-term fasts. Our body's preferred energy source is glucose (sugar), which we store as glycogen in our liver and muscles. When we are fasting, our body uses the stored glycogen to get the energy we need. Once the stored glycogen is used up, typically after twenty-four to forty-eight hours, our body starts burning fat for fuel, turning fat into glucose and molecules known as ketones. Using fat for energy is known as ketosis (the basis of the ketogenic diet).

FAST-MIMICKING DIET

Dr. Valter Longo from the University of Southern California, referenced in one of the studies above, has created a fast-mimicking diet (FMD). You can read about the diet in his book *The Longevity Diet*. His FMD is a five-day program that provides a small number of calories each day so that participants will stick with it. Dr. Longo believes that most of the cell rejuvenation benefits from fasting do not occur until after three to four days, yet most people cannot make it that long with a pure water fast. By allowing a small number of calories over those five days, the FMD allows the body to get into the cell rejuvenation stage. For people who do not want to prepare meals during the FMD, he also offers five-day meal kits and donates all sales proceeds to charity.

I use his FMD kits every few months. It is a great way to rejuvenate the body and start fresh again. I find it particularly helpful after returning from a vacation or trip, when I was not as diligent about my eating habits.

EPIGENETIC AGE

Are you curious why older people are prone to more negative outcomes if they catch COVID-19, the regular flu, or other viruses? It is because the immune cells needed to mount an effective response to these viruses decrease in our blood as we age. This is called immunosenescence. The process of immunosenescence leads to higher viral infection rates as well as higher incidents of cancer and autoimmune diseases.[11]

Epigenetics is the study of how our behavior and environment can cause changes that affect the way our genes work. Epigenetics is a major factor in aging, and there is a company that offers epigenetic age reports calculated by a simple blood test.

TruDiagnostic™, based in Lexington, Kentucky, developed the TruAge™ collection of tests which can determine your epigenetic (biological) age by reporting on how "old" your cells and DNA look, including your immune cells. "Younger" immune cells should help put off many age-related ailments and diseases.

The TruAge test provides a wealth of information for a cost of $499.

Here is one page of the results from my most recent test.

YOUR EXTRINSIC
Epigenetic Age

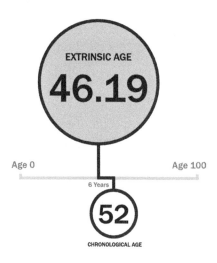

Your measurement of
Extrinsic Epigenetic Age
is 46.19 years

My chronological age at the time of the test was 52, but my epigenetic age was 46.

You can learn more about TruDiagnostic at https://trudiagnostic.com/.

BIOLOGICAL AGE RESOURCES

1. Here are two online sources available to help approximate your biological age via lifestyle questions:
   https://www.health.com/beauty/quiz-discover-your-real-age
   https://www.mymathtables.com/calculator/age/human/biological-human-age-calculator.html

2. Here is an online source to approximate biological age by your heart rate and VO$_2$ Max: https://www.worldfitnesslevel.org/#/

3. Here is an alternative source to TruDiagnostic™ to approximate biological age by blood test: https://www.viome.com/test-your-biological-age-with-health-intelligence

4. For up-to-date online resources and current web links, please visit our website at www.Section16Secrets.com.

We know that an active lifestyle and a positive mindset are significant contributors to longevity. Medical care, for both prevention and treatment, is also essential. Retired Section 16 officers typically have the financial capability to acquire the best medical care.

Why do some affluent individuals take advantage of what medical science provides and others do not? Let us explore that in our next chapter.

CHAPTER 13

THE HEALTHSPAN EXTENDER MINDSET

SICKCARE, HEALTHCARE, AND OPTIMIZATION

"Being rich is having money; being wealthy is having time."

—MARGARET BONNANO

Many Section 16 officers have accumulated significant wealth. For some, it has come at the expense of their long-term health. These officers work long hours, usually in stressful situations. They travel to different time zones, eat on the run, and even on their days off, are rarely "unplugged."

Tom and Sarah have the financial resources to provide for themselves for the rest of their lives, but how long will that be?

Silica-Corp offers significant healthcare benefits to their Section 16 officers, including executive physicals on an annual basis.

Executive physicals are deep-dive medical examinations, typically lasting several hours to as long as two days. The executive physicals will cover a battery of tests designed to assist with the early detection of heart disease, vascular blockages, diabetes, cancer, and other ailments. Treatments for many disorders have a high degree of success when started early.

Many of the major US hospitals and research centers offer executive physicals. What makes them popular is that the executive travels to one medical center and gets all the various tests completed the same day. A general practitioner might order multiple tests at a regular physical, but each of those tests must be scheduled with different labs or specialists. Getting the test results, and then interpreting those results, can take weeks.

Because of the one-stop-shop nature of the executive physical, it offers significant advantages over a fifteen-minute annual checkup with a local doctor. However, all physicals—executive or traditional—have one thing in common: They are searching for signs of disease. Absent any evidence of disease, a clean bill of health is issued and the patient is told to come back next year. Treatment for any illness begins if or when proof of disease is present.

This "looking for disease" system is not *healthcare*. It is *sickcare*. The absence of disease does not mean you are healthy—it means you are not at the stage where an illness requires treatment. This traditional medical model is *re*active, not *pro*active.

A growing number of physicians and medical centers have transitioned from the traditional sickcare mindset to one of healthcare and optimization.

I reviewed some of these medical centers with Tom and Sarah, and they were intrigued. They started researching different optimization physicians on their own and thought they found a good match. There were three problems, though:

1. The physician was located out of state
2. The physician did not accept their Silica-Corp insurance
3. Even if the physician did accept their insurance, Silica-Corp's plan provided reimbursement for only traditional sickcare tests and treatment protocols.

Tom told me they would schedule the traditional executive physical that Silica-Corp covered, but then he would start pushing their executive benefits group to offer more.

I asked Tom what he would do if Silica-Corp never offered programs outside of the traditional "sickcare" model. Would he continue visiting physicians who were looking for only disease, or would he find a way to optimize his health and longevity?

Tom said he had not thought that far ahead. He planned to take advantage of what was available to him now and lobby for changes to his company plan that might benefit him later.

That is where our thinking differs, I told him. These physicians and services *are* available to you now. *You* have the financial resources to hire any physician in the world. Once you embrace the mindset that *you* are responsible for your health, optimization, and longevity, your company health insurance and benefits plan no longer matter. I call this mindset *The Healthspan Extender*.

THE HEALTHSPAN EXTENDER

Tom and Sarah have accumulated a net worth of $15 million. It is plenty to provide for their post-Silica-Corp years. What if they allocated just 1 percent of their net worth as an annual budget to focus on their healthcare, optimization, and longevity? They need to view this 1 percent allocation as an investment, not an expense. It's an investment in extending their healthspan, not just their lifespan. It's an investment that helps them to "buy back" some of the health they may have lost along their journey in corporate America.

A 1 percent budget seems small in percentage terms. Still, when you apply that percentage to a $15 million net worth, it allows for $150,000 of the best physicians, clinics, personal trainers, nutritionists, chefs, and equipment on an annual basis. The larger your net worth, the more likely your personal *Healthspan Extender* will cost half a percent of your net worth or less.

I explained to Tom and Sarah that for a budget of no more than 1 percent of their net worth, they could gain access to some of the best healthcare providers and programs in the world, without ever worrying about what Silica-Corp will or will not cover.

Tom's personal *Healthspan Extender* will look different from others, but some of the common components might be:

- Longevity physicians and concierge medicine
- Full body scans
- Genetic testing
- Supplements
- Hormone replacement therapy (HRT)
- Personal trainers, nutritionists, and chefs

- Equipment
- Tracking

LONGEVITY PHYSICIANS AND CONCIERGE MEDICINE

Concierge medicine is a relationship with a physician outside of a traditional insurance plan. You pay an annual retainer fee for (almost) immediate access to your physician, and your doctor is available for phone calls, text messages, and face-to-face (or virtual) meetings on short notice. The concierge physician will work with a limited number of patients to spend an adequate amount of time with each.

Most of us have experienced the opposite in the traditional sickcare industry. Due to declining reimbursement rates and pressure from insurance companies, conventional sickcare physicians must see multiple patients per hour, so their visits are swift. With so many patients to tend to, they are usually booked out several days (or weeks) in advance. When the day of the appointment arrives, patients spend ten minutes waiting in the exam room, fifteen minutes with the nurse, and then another ten minutes with the physician. Your entire visit is over just inside of thirty minutes.

Longevity physicians tend to work in the concierge model. Their specialty is to dive deeper with their patients to optimize their health and performance. Longevity physicians can be your "team leader" for four of the pillars of *The Healthspan Extender*: full body scans, genetic testing, hormone replacement, and supplements.

FULL BODY SCANS

If you have ever known a young(ish) stroke victim, you were probably surprised when you heard the news. "Uncle John had a stroke? I thought he was healthy. He is only 60 years old." The same thing when a heart attack strikes. "Aunt Joan runs every day. How did she have a heart attack at age 55?"

You then learn John's carotid artery was 80 percent blocked or Joan needs bypass surgery. In both instances, vascular system blockages incapacitate seemingly healthy people with little or no warning.

Longevity physicians, and some executive physicals, will offer full body scans to detect potential vascular issues early. Most physicians in the traditional sickcare model do not provide imaging until there is evidence of symptoms. By then, it may be too late.

Full body scans can also determine your bone density and how much visceral fat (the dangerous fat around your organs) you are carrying. These scans become a baseline for monitoring progress as well as keeping a closer eye on potential issues as you age.

GENETIC TESTING

What if your genetic makeup puts you at a higher risk for certain diseases or cancer down the road? Having that knowledge today allows you to take preventive steps early.

I was hesitant to learn about my genetic makeup. What if I was at a higher risk of Alzheimer's disease? How would I process that information? If I misplaced my car keys in the future or forgot to pay a property tax bill on time, would I immediately think I was losing my memory? I was concerned about the anxiety that could produce.

I was chatting with Dan Sullivan at a Strategic Coach® workshop about that anxiety, and he had a great take on it:

> Me: I am impressed with all the testing available for people concerned about their longevity, but part of me is nervous to learn about my future vulnerabilities.
>
> Dan: Well, everyone finds out.
>
> Me: I know many people are comfortable knowing. I am just nervous about how I would react if I found something wrong.
>
> Dan: Everyone finds out.
>
> Me: I am not sure if I want to be part of that group that finds out.
>
> Dan: *Everyone. Finds. Out.* The tests are just an issue of timing. Whether you have the tests or not. *Everyone* finds out. If you are predisposed to particular problems or diseases, you will *eventually* find out. The question should be, do you want to find out when you still have time to try to course-correct?

A longtime friend and client had recently passed away from amyotrophic lateral sclerosis (ALS). He was one of the most athletic and healthy-looking people I knew, and once the disease hit, he was gone in just a few months. Another friend and client went out for a jog one morning like he did every morning, and a heart attack hit. He never came home. If either had a chance to go back in time, would they have liked to know if they were predisposed to particular issues?

I think they would have. I know the families they left behind would have supported that decision. Everything seems so clear once we have the benefit of hindsight.

Genetic testing not only helps you understand and prepare for potential issues in the future, but testing can also help optimize your health and performance today. Certain gene patterns might suggest you are more of an endurance athlete than a power athlete. You might get more value from exercising in cold weather than in warm weather. Certain genetic traits can make someone more susceptible to tendon issues or rotator cuff issues, too. Would that not be helpful to know before you start a weightlifting program?

Your genetic makeup can even assist with weight loss. Certain genes make it more challenging to lose weight. You probably know someone who can eat a pint of ice cream every evening, and they never seem to gain weight. Others have a single breadstick with dinner and then gain two pounds by morning. The simplest way to lose weight is to reduce the calories you are consuming, but your genetic profile helps determine how quickly you burn calories and your desire to eat certain food types.

Studies have shown that the human salivary alpha-amylase gene (AMY1) can influence how effectively individuals process starchy carbohydrates. As humans have evolved, multiple copies of this gene have become present in our systems. The average copy number is six, but it can range from a single copy to over twenty. Studies suggest that the more copies of the AMY1 gene in our bodies, the greater our ability to tolerate and digest starchy carbohydrates.[12]

I was amazed to learn that my genetic profile showed I had only two copies of the AMY1 gene. This means that I have difficulty processing starchy carbohydrates, and I have a higher risk and predisposition to obesity. I also have a higher risk of insulin resistance and diabetes if I consume a high-starch carbohydrate diet.

When I lost 124 pounds over 294 days, it was before I learned of my genetic profile. I achieved that through a combination of weight training, cardio exercise, and ketogenic (low carbohydrate) eating. At the time, I had no idea how many copies of the AMY1 gene I had. All I knew was that ketogenic eating worked for me. Imagine how much easier my journey would have been if I knew the genetic deck I was playing with was "stacked against me" if I ate too many carbs. Once I saw my genetic profile, a lot of things in my life "made sense."

Here is the copy of my personal "CarbChoice" report showing my two copies of the AMY1 gene:

CarbChoice

William, here is your CarbChoice result indicating that you are a Low Range Starch Carbohydrate processor.

Classified in this CarbChoice report as the population group most likely to have poor capacity to process starchy carbohydrates.

Your lower processing capacity means:

- You may not produce as much of the enzyme in your saliva needed to break down the starch found in carbohydrates.

- You may have reduced tolerance of high-starch diets.

- You may be at a higher risk of, and predisposition to, obesity.

- You may have reduced glycaemic control resulting in decreased glucose or blood sugar control.

- You may have an increased risk of metabolic abnormalities which occur when the normal process of metabolism is or becomes disrupted.

- You may be at increased risk of obesity compared to individuals with a higher processing result.

- You may be at higher risk of insulin resistance and diabetes if you are consuming a high starch carbohydrate diet.

Dietary Recommendations

Your low starch carbohydrate processing capacity means you should aim to avoid refined and processed starchy carbohydrates in your everyday diet.

Trial a low carbohydrate diet providing 25% of overall daily energy intake (approx. 165g for men) made up of low starch options.

Lifestyle Recommendations

You should undertake moderate to high-intensity physical activity. Before starting this type of exercise, you should discuss this with your fitness or health practitioner, especially if suffering from any medical condition or injury.

Your longevity physician can order the appropriate genetic tests and assist you with interpreting the results.

SUPPLEMENTS

Many people take a multivitamin each day, and that is helpful. Have you ever been tested for specific vitamin deficiencies? What are your vitamin B or D levels?

You can guess and read something online that says, "Vitamin D is helpful for a strong immune system," but how much do *you* need? Are you aware of the importance of a lesser-known vitamin, K2 (MK7), and how it works alongside vitamin D?

Your longevity physician can prescribe a supplement regimen for your personal physiological needs based on the proper testing.

Supplements do not stop with just vitamins. Are you deficient in any amino acids, such as L-arginine, L-lysine, L-proline, or L-theanine? Amino acids assist almost every system throughout our bodies. They help maintain muscle and tissue strength, healing and repair, normal digestion, hormone regulation, healthy skin, hair, and nails and dealing with anxiety and stress.

How about minerals? Our bodies use minerals for many different jobs. We need macrominerals such as calcium, chloride, magnesium, phosphorus, potassium, sodium, and sulfur, including others, to keep our heart, brain, muscles, and bones working correctly. There are also trace minerals, such as cobalt, copper, iodine, iron, manganese, selenium, and zinc.

Not all cars require the same maintenance, and not all bodies need the same care. If you put 5w30 oil in a vehicle that requires 10w40 oil, you may see a drop in performance. If you put diesel fuel in a car that requires unleaded gasoline, the engine might get permanently damaged.

A supplement plan crafted specifically for your physiological needs can help ensure you perform at your best.

HORMONE REPLACEMENT THERAPY

Aging is inevitable, but symptoms associated with aging do not have to be. Male and female hormone levels naturally fluctuate throughout life. As we age, those fluctuations become more severe.

Women experience menopause, a reduction in estrogen and progesterone production, while men experience andropause, a reduction in testosterone production.

As hormone levels drop, both women and men can experience fatigue, a loss of energy, irritability, depression, decreased muscle mass and strength, reduced bone density with an increased risk of osteoporosis, and reduced libido.

It is not only estrogen, progesterone, and testosterone that decrease as we age. Both women and men can suffer from reduced thyroid function, known as hypothyroidism. Low thyroid can result in low energy, weight gain, and moodiness.

As a culture, we seem to accept low energy, a depleted libido, weight gain, muscle loss, and all the other symptoms of reduced hormonal output as a function of aging. It does not have to be that way.

Hormone replacement therapy (HRT) works to restore hormone levels to where they were before the onset of menopause and andropause. By stimulating hormone production, it is possible to reduce the adverse effects of aging and improve the quality of life.

Some of the benefits of HRT:

- Improved energy levels
- Stabilized emotional state, reduced moodiness
- Improved muscle tone and physical fitness
- Stronger bones
- Improved sleep, with relief from hot flashes and night sweats
- Increased libido

Although I have referenced many positive aspects of HRT, I cannot stress enough the importance of working closely with a physician who specializes in these therapies. It is essential to have your blood and hormone levels tested regularly to help catch potential side effects or unintended consequences early. HRT is not a "set it and forget it" process.

Some people have no interest in optimizing their hormone levels to feel great. I have heard people say, "If I start taking hormones, I'll have to take them for the rest of my life." That might be true, but would that not be a better solution than remaining deficient for the rest of your life?

Many insurance plans will not cover HRT, but that should not be a roadblock for you. Using the mindset of *The Healthspan Extender* and allocating 1 percent of your net worth, you should have plenty of room in your budget for these therapies.

Discuss HRT with your longevity physician to see if it might benefit you.

PROFESSIONAL SERVICES: PERSONAL TRAINERS, NUTRITIONISTS, AND CHEFS

If you spend thirty minutes a day on the treadmill, you will improve your cardiovascular fitness. If you get in the habit of doing fifty push-ups every day, you will expand your upper body strength. If you make a conscious effort to reduce the amount of sugar you ingest, you will reduce your risk of diabetes later in life. If you reduce or eliminate fast food and eat most of your meals at home, you will eat better quality food and improve your health.

Nothing I just described should surprise anyone. Whether I surveyed 100 or 1,000 people, I think most adults would be able to verbalize the benefits of the treadmill, push-ups, reduced sugar intake, and eliminating fast food.

If we all know the answers, why do so many people resist doing what they know will benefit them? Lack of accountability.

PERSONAL TRAINERS

As part of *The Healthspan Extender*, anyone serious about improving their health and longevity should hire a personal trainer. Your trainer will not only prescribe a program unique to your goals; they will hold you accountable. Something as simple as scheduling a time to work out once or twice per week will put you on a path for success.

When you are in complete control of your schedule, it is easy to let the "fire of the day" take over and push other activities aside. If you planned to work out at 4:00 p.m., but you have a critical email to take care of, it is easy to push 4:00 p.m. back to 5:00 p.m. Perhaps 5:00 p.m. becomes 8:00 p.m., and at some point, you decide, "It is too late, and I am too tired," and the workout is canceled.

If you had an appointment scheduled to meet with your trainer at 4:00 p.m., you are more likely to keep that appointment and not let other issues derail your workout plans. Someone else is counting on you to show up for that appointment. This layer of accountability does not mean you can never reschedule a training session, but you are less likely to make a *habit* of missing your workout time. Instead, your habit becomes, "I work out every Monday and Friday at 4:00 p.m."

DIETITIANS AND NUTRITIONISTS

Dietitians and nutritionists can also hold you accountable. Both professionals have specialized training to coach you about dietary needs. Registered dietitians are also trained to diagnose and treat eating disorders.

Your dietitian, nutritionist, or longevity physician can assist with food testing to determine what types of food might negatively affect you. Testing can take all the guesswork out of your meal planning. Your dietitian or nutritionist can provide recipes for you and customized shopping lists. With concierge-type professionals, you can even text them a photo of a food label while shopping to get their feedback.

If you know you have an event being held at a restaurant this weekend, you can review the menu in advance with your dietitian or nutritionist to help determine the best choices for your body.

Most relationships include regular calls or meetings to hold you accountable and plan for the weeks ahead.

PERSONAL CHEFS

Your dietitian or nutritionist might provide great advice, recipes, and shopping lists, but what if you do not have the time to cook healthier food? You are running late on your way home from work, so you stop at the grocery store to pick up a platter of something prepared.

For some people, a personal chef sounds like an extravagant expenditure. They picture someone in a white coat spending hours in the kitchen and then a butler in a tuxedo serving them from large silver platters. Those personal services do exist but more so in the movies than in real life. Those professionals are *private chefs* who serve one family as their full-time job.

Personal chefs work for multiple families, and there are personal chef services available for reasonable costs.

According to the US Department of Agriculture, families with children spend an average of forty-four minutes a day preparing, serving, and cleaning up after meals.[13] This daily ritual is more than 267 hours annually!

For some high-net-worth families, a personal chef's benefit is not only for the nutritional value but also for the time savings they provide. Is it worth it to you to "buy back" those 267 hours each year?

Most chefs will charge by the meal. Some will prepare everything at your home, and some will prepare the meals in their commercial kitchen and then deliver them to you ready to reheat. Chefs will work with your nutritionist on meal planning, and they take care of the grocery shopping, food preparation, and best of all, the cleanup afterward.

The cost for personal chefs will vary by region, but for five dinners each week, for a family of four, the price should range between $250 and $350, excluding the cost of groceries. You will receive quality meals tailored to your dietary needs, and you will "buy back" the time associated with shopping, preparing, and cleaning up after meals.

The Healthspan Extender mindset opened a lot of opportunities for Tom and Sarah. They just needed to think about things differently. Tom and Sarah now realized they had the financial resources to transition away from the sickcare model of medicine to one of true healthcare and optimization. In our next chapter, we'll review some of the tools Tom and Sarah can consider as part of their personal *Healthspan Extender*.

CHAPTER 14

TOOLS FOR THE BODY AND MIND

"Do something today that your future self will thank you for."

—SEAN PATRICK FLANNERY

Tom and Sarah have followed the *Section 16 GPS* process and have amplified their wealth, accumulating significant assets. They have now decided to research longevity physicians and use their wealth to start on the path toward their personal *Healthspan Extender*.

The longevity physician they choose will assist them with their full body scans, genetic testing, and individual hormone and supplement routines. Their personal trainer will help them build muscle mass and bone density as they age, and their nutritionist and chef will help keep their family healthy and allow them to buy back the time previously spent shopping and preparing meals.

The Healthspan Extender mindset will also provide Tom and Sarah with a budget to invest in equipment and memberships to improve their health and longevity. A treadmill or some dumbbells is a nice addition to your home gym, but there are many other tools you can invest in for both your body and your mind.

I utilize all the products discussed below.

HORMESIS AND SAUNAS

You may have heard the saying, "Whatever doesn't kill me makes me stronger." That is hormesis.

Hormesis is a good level of stress. A moderate amount of stress is positive for our bodies and minds, whereas a large amount of the same stressor could be lethal. Hormesis allows our bodies to build an adaptive stress response, where we can benefit from stress in low doses. Exercise is a form of hormesis. You must damage your muscles via weightlifting so that your body can repair and build them back even stronger.

Exposure to extreme heat or cold for a short amount of time is another form of hormesis. If you wander unprotected in the desert heat for five days, you might die. If you expose yourself to extreme heat for just thirty minutes, your body will become more resilient toward that type of stress in the future.

Sweating for therapeutic purposes is not new. The ancient Mayan culture used sweat boxes over 3,000 years ago. Early Greeks and Romans built elaborate steam baths.

If you have ever visited a spa or a higher-end gym, I am sure you have tried a modern-day sauna.

After fifteen to twenty minutes of sweating, you emerge more relaxed and rested. Any muscle soreness has improved, and you will probably sleep better that evening.

For the past three decades, researchers in Finland have studied the effects of saunas on thousands of Finnish men and women, and the results are impressive. Men who used a sauna two to three times per week for approximately fifteen minutes showed a 22 percent reduction in sudden cardiac death than those who used a sauna only *once* per week. Men who went four to seven times per week were 63 percent less likely to die from a sudden heart attack and 50 percent less likely to die from other cardiovascular diseases than those who used a sauna only once per week.

Some think that the relaxation benefits of sauna use contribute to a reduced risk of neurological issues such as dementia. Those who used a sauna two to three times per week were 22 percent less likely to experience dementia than those who did not use a sauna. For participants who used a sauna four to seven times per week, the risk of dementia dropped 66 percent.[14]

Although this study followed over 2,000 participants for twenty years, more research is needed to solidify the neurological benefits of sauna use.

For the cardiovascular benefits, the cause and effect is clearer. As our body temperature increases, blood moves from our core to our skin to facilitate sweating, and our heart beats faster to move more blood to increase our sweating. Some sauna users will experience a heart rate of up to 150 beats per minute, like moderate-intensity exercise. This "exercise substitute" has also been shown to improve HRV and blood pressure.

The body releases heat shock proteins as our core temperature rises. These proteins help reduce inflammation, which is why muscle soreness improves after sauna use.

The Finnish study utilized traditional dry-heat saunas. A dry-heat sauna heats the air in the room up to 195°F. For home use, many people have chosen to install an infrared sauna.

Infrared saunas utilize infrared *wavelengths* to heat our bodies, instead of the air. Infrared heat lamps can generate near-infrared, mid-infrared, or far-infrared wavelengths. Each type of wavelength penetrates our skin and bodies differently.

The sun generates all colors of the rainbow and a combination of visible and invisible light. Not all light is beneficial. Too much sunlight will damage our skin. Infrared heat provides many of the benefits of sun exposure without the dangers of solar radiation.

Traditional dry saunas heat our bodies indirectly. Dry saunas must heat the air first and then rely on convection (air currents) to move the hot air to our bodies. Once the heated air touches our skin, conduction takes over, and our skin absorbs the heat. There is heat loss between the convection and conduction stages, so traditional saunas must be heated to 150°F–195°F. Some people have difficulty breathing when the air is so hot (it can make the lungs feel like they're burning), resulting in shorter sauna sessions.

Infrared saunas transfer more heat directly to the body, so the sauna temperature can be set to 100°F–160°F, allowing you to tolerate an extended session.

You can purchase an infrared sauna in the range of $2,000–$8,000, depending on the size. Some saunas fit one person, and others can accommodate three or more people at once.

We purchased a three-person sauna, but our family has never had more than two people in it at a time. It is just nice to have the extra space.

Resist the urge to look on Amazon for the lowest cost sauna. You want to make sure your sauna uses high-quality infrared lamps and emits a low amount of electric and magnetic fields (EMF) radiation. Most high-quality saunas generate EMFs at or below the level of everyday household items such as a hairdryer or blender.

HORMESIS AND CRYOTHERAPY

Exposure to cold is a different type of hormesis. If you wandered unprotected in Antarctica for five days, the extreme cold would kill you. If your exposure to extreme cold lasted for only a few minutes, your body would trigger another adaptive stress response.

Sauna use releases heat shock proteins, and your blood flows from your interior to your extremities to promote sweating. The opposite occurs with frigid temperatures, and cold shock proteins are released. When our brain senses rapid heat transfer from our skin, our sympathetic nervous system takes over, and we enter a fight-or-flight mode with our circulatory system. Our vascular system constricts, and our body starts to pull blood away from our extremities to reduce our heat loss. That blood is sent to our core to protect our internal organs from this cold stress. As blood pools in our core, it is oxygenated and enriched with nutrients.

Once you remove the external cold stress, vasodilation occurs, and our brain releases that blood supply in our core to quickly flow back to our extremities.

Hippocrates discussed the benefits of cold-water bathing, so this therapy is not new. Cold-water immersion has been prescribed throughout history for ailments from bruises to depression to hysteria.[15] You have probably seen athletes immersed in ice baths to reduce inflammation after a competition.

Although the science behind cold shock is well known, it is difficult for many people to achieve the benefits. Quite simply, it is uncomfortable. Some consider the heat shock received via sauna use relaxing. That is not the case with cold showers, ice baths, and polar plunges. When you are not looking forward to something and you know it will be stressful, it is easy to take it off your personal health menu.

Cryotherapy chambers allow you to benefit from cold stress hormesis in a short duration—typically just three minutes. The air inside the cryo chamber is cooled with liquid nitrogen, down to –150°F to –200°F. You stand in the cryo chamber, and your body is exposed to the cold air from your shoulders down.

How can you survive at −200°F for even a short period? Because you are in cold air and not cold water. The dry cold created by the cryotherapy chamber cools the skin but does not generate the penetrating cold that an ice bath will. With an ice bath, your muscle tissue will start to congeal and freeze, resulting in a "stiff" feeling and temporary loss of muscle function. It also takes fifteen to twenty minutes or more of an ice bath to generate the same benefits that can come from just three minutes in the cryo chamber.

I have used cryotherapy on a semi-regular basis, and I always feel exhilarated and refreshed after just three minutes.

Cryo chambers can be prohibitively expensive for home use. In addition to the chamber's up-front cost, you will have ongoing expenses for the liquid nitrogen used to cool the air. Unlike saunas that are perfectly safe for solo use, cryotherapy sessions need to be monitored by a partner. For these reasons, you should consider a membership to a spa or gym that offers cryotherapy sessions. Some locations provide unlimited cryo sessions for $150–$250 per month or individual sessions for $25–$50 per visit.

INTERACTIVE EXERCISE EQUIPMENT

You have probably seen the Peloton commercials of someone riding on a stationary bike being motivated by a trainer on the screen. Some look at interactive training as more of a gimmick—having a "buddy" to ride along with you. Science tells a different story.

If you are riding your bike alone or walking or running on

your treadmill in the basement, it is easy to cut your workout short. After all, you did *something* that day. Who will know the difference?

What if you use your treadmill in a group class, whether that class is live or prerecorded? Will you stop your workout ten minutes early when you are so close to finishing?

According to a study by the Society of Behavioral Medicine, researchers found that people who worked out with a partner committed to their exercise for longer than those who worked out alone. Those working out in a group setting improved their overall performance and doubled their workout time compared to those who exercised by themselves.[16]

Companies like Peloton and iFit (by NordicTrack) help otherwise solo exercisers increase their strength and stamina through what psychologists call the Köhler motivation gain effect. The Köhler effect is a phenomenon that occurs when a person works harder as a member of a group compared to working alone. For example, a team climbing Mount Kilimanjaro cannot ascend the mountain faster than the slowest climber in their group. Köhler discovered that lower-performing team members, the "weak links," tend to exert additional effort when part of a team.

The same phenomenon applies to interactive workouts. Both Peloton and iFit will show "leaderboards" as you exercise. For some of you, the competitive spirit takes over when you see your name at the end of the leaderboard. You may not have the skills to be the best competitor out of the 500 individuals who have completed a particular bike route or run, but you may have the skills to improve your performance and move from

500 up to 450. If you're really motivated, you may even be able to break the top ten.

Researchers at Kansas State University tested this theory in 2012. For the first part of their research, they studied participants on a stationary exercise bike for six sessions over four weeks. Their instructions were to simply ride the bike for as long as they could.

For the second part of the study, researchers paired riders with a partner. Riders were told their partners were riding in another room and were given a video screen where they could watch each other. However, their partners were actually prerecorded videos.

At the end of the exercise, researchers told participants their partner had also participated in the first part of the study and ridden the bike for approximately 40 percent *longer* than they had. Riders were tricked into believing their partners were just a little bit better than they were, which motivated the riders. When riding with a partner, they rode 90 percent longer (on average) than when they rode alone. When partners who performed at a higher level were introduced, the participants worked harder.

Finally, for stage three of this study, participants were told they would be teamed up with their virtual partners to generate a team score. The team score would be the time of the person who rode the shortest distance. In other words, the person who quit first.

In the first part of the study, participants believed their partners rode longer than they had. When riders were a part of a team, they rode approximately two minutes longer than when they were competing against a virtual partner. Participants did not want to let their partner down or be the first person to quit. Researchers created a narrative where the participant believed they were the "weak link" so they pushed themselves further.

By the study's end, riders on a team rode approximately 160 percent longer than those in the partner group alone and almost 200 percent longer than riders who exercised independently.[17]

It can be challenging to find a workout partner willing to go running in the dead of winter. It can also be hard to find a partner eager to ride a stationary bike alongside you in your basement. Interactive companies such as Peloton and iFit allow you to work out with partners and trainers, from around the world, on your schedule.

Excluding the equipment cost (bike or treadmill), subscriptions to Peloton and iFit currently cost $15–$40 per month.

SLEEP COOLING TECHNOLOGY

Before reviewing the cool technology (pun intended) available, let us examine the benefits of a cooler sleeping environment.

Adults who get less than seven hours of sleep each night are more likely to report health problems, including heart attack, asthma, and depression. Lack of sleep can also impact our blood pressure. During normal sleep, your blood pressure goes down. If you are not sleeping well and for long enough, your blood pressure stays higher for a more extended amount of time.

Researchers have found that sleeping in a cooler environment can improve sleep quality and allow more deep sleep to be achieved. During slow-wave deep sleep, most of the body's restorative functions occur. Metabolic rate, heart rate, and oxygen consumption decreases, and your cells have time to recover from the day's stress.[18]

Our body regulates our core temperature via the hypothalamus and will range between 96.8°F and 100.4°F during each twenty-four-hour cycle. A warmer core temperature is associated with being awake, alert, and energetic. A cooler core temperature is associated with drowsiness and sleep.

If you can reduce the temperature of your sleeping environment, you might achieve one or more of these five benefits:

1. **Fall asleep faster.** A cooler room helps the body lower its core temperature, naturally signaling that it is time for sleep.
2. **Reduce insomnia.** Researchers have found that people with insomnia have a higher core body temperature. They stay awake while their bodies lose the heat that interrupts their sleep. If you can lower your core temperature more quickly, you can fall asleep or remain asleep with fewer interruptions.
3. **More consistent sleep cycles.** Sleeping in a cooler environment helps you stay asleep without interrupting your sleep cycles. When your body temperature is too high during the night, you are more likely to wake up, or you might start sweating. Sweat is the body's way to cool itself naturally, but it does not make for a pleasant sleep experience.
4. **Improved hormone production.** Human growth hormone is produced during sleep. So is melatonin. You have probably seen melatonin supplements that help people fall asleep

faster, but the body's *natural* production of melatonin can help you stay asleep throughout the night. Melatonin production increases in a cool environment.

5. **Increased metabolism and weight loss.** A study has shown sleeping at a cooler temperature reduces the amount of "white fat" in our bodies while increasing "brown fat." White fat is stored for extra energy and builds up in obesity. Brown fat breaks down blood sugar (glucose) to create heat and maintain our body temperature. Researchers observed participants for four months sleeping in temperature-controlled rooms. After a month of sleeping at 66°F, their volume of brown fat (the good fat) increased 42 percent. Their amount of white fat (belly fat) decreased.[19]

Sleeping cold does not mean you are "shivering." Even a moderately cold environment can produce these results.

You can achieve a cooler sleep environment by setting your thermostat to 60°F–68°F. For most homes, this is not energy efficient. If you have central air-conditioning, you are cooling your entire house to this temperature, yet you sleep only in your bedroom.

Some companies offer bed cooling devices that allow you to maintain a set temperature for just your sleeping area—your bed.

ChiliPad™ is a liquid-cooled mattress topper. Water has natural thermal advantages for both cooling and heating. The radiator in your car moves coolant through its system so heat can flow to the air outside. The ChiliPad moves water through thin tubes embedded in the mattress topper to reduce the temperature of your bed. You can set the temperature as low as 55°F, but in practice, the system will produce a reduction of approximately 15°F below the ambient air temperature in your room.

You can adjust the ChiliPad settings for both sides of the bed separately, so your partner has independent control of their temperature. I have used the ChiliPad for two years and have been pleased with the results.

BedJet™ is an air-controlled mattress cooling system. A fan blows cool air in between your sheets to help dissipate heat.

Other companies offer similar technology, and most companies will allow for significant trial periods of thirty to one hundred nights. You can expect to pay somewhere between $400 and $700, depending on the brand and your bed size.

FLOAT TANKS

Saunas and cryotherapy help promote recovery and longevity by *stressing* our bodies. It is also important to *relax* our bodies (and minds).

Float tanks are sensory-deprivation chambers used for restricted environmental stimulation therapy (REST). The tanks are about double the size of a standard bathtub, filled with approximately ten to twelve inches of water heated to body temperature. The water is saturated with 900–1,200 pounds of Epsom salt (magnesium sulfate), making floating effortless.

When you lie down in the tank and close the lid, all outside stimulation ceases, including sound, light, and gravity. You are wrapped in your own cocoon of warmth and silence. As you float in a state of weightlessness, quiet, and darkness, your brain enters a deeply relaxed state.

Floating for mind and body benefits is not new. People have made pilgrimages to the Dead Sea for centuries to float in its incredibly salty water. Over the past decade, float tanks have become more mainstream, with many spas and gyms offering floating services.

FOUR BENEFITS OF FLOATING

1. **A reduction in cortisol and stress hormone production.** Floating decreases anxiety and stress. In one study, participants who floated for twelve sessions reported reduced stress, anxiety, and depression as well as improved sleep.[20]
2. **Improved sleep.** People have reported falling asleep easier on days they have used a float tank, and they have reported a higher quality sleep. They wake up feeling more rested than usual. Part of this comes from reducing cortisol and a general sense of relaxation. Some people believe the water's high magnesium concentration is partially absorbed, improving sleep. However, there is ongoing scientific debate about how effectively magnesium can be absorbed through the skin.
3. **Relief of physical pain.** The weightless environment removes all physical stress from our bodies, reducing muscle and joint pain. For athletes, floating improves recovery after workouts by reducing lactic acid in the blood. In a weightless environment, lactic acid moves out of the muscles more quickly, reducing muscle stiffness and pain.
4. **Reset our sympathetic nervous system.** Our brains spend a lot of time in the fight-or-flight mode during the day. We

might not be running from a saber-toothed tiger all day long, but we are worried about getting to work on time, not getting a speeding ticket, performing well in a client meeting, paying our bills on time, helping our children with homework, and so on. The float tank is a warm and relaxing environment, probably not much different from the womb. This atmosphere downregulates our sympathetic nervous system, reducing cortisol levels. Our parasympathetic nervous system activates, elevating dopamine levels and releasing endorphins—the neurotransmitters of happiness.

You might wonder, could you not get the same benefits from a nice long nap? When we lie on a mattress, we are aware of our body weight, and we must constantly adjust our bodies to get comfortable. Without fighting gravity in the float tank, our muscles, joints, and bones all get a well-deserved break. Our bodies now have a ton of extra resources previously used for supporting our weight (and running from the occasional saber-toothed tiger) now directed toward healing, rest, and recovery.

Float tanks for home use can cost between $10,000 and $30,000. A sixty- to ninety-minute float session at a local gym or spa can cost $45–$75. Many float centers offer monthly packages of unlimited float sessions for $200–$300.

BRAIN BIOHACKING

You can utilize several less expensive tools as part of *The Healthspan Extender* that do not involve a $6,000 sauna or $20,000 float tank.

As discussed in previous sections, it is just as important to take care of your mind as it is your body. Many people, especially those with stressful careers, such as Section 16 officers, tend to have an upregulated sympathetic nervous system. They spend more time in fight-or-flight mode than the rest-and-digest mode of the parasympathetic nervous system.

Sometimes it can be difficult to "shut off" the mind to move into a relaxation state. Every day, some "fire" in the business world needs to be extinguished.

Here are three inexpensive tools you can consider to assist with your transition to a state of increased mindfulness and relaxation.

MEDITATION APPS

We are used to our phones being a distraction. Meditation apps allow you to use your phone for something positive—they guide you through various meditations to train your brain to focus on the moment. Three popular apps are Headspace, Calm, and Insight Timer.

In a 2018 study, researchers tested Headspace with sixty-nine adults. The study started with participants answering questions about their mental state—their positive and negative feelings, stress levels, and irritability over the previous week. Over the next month, half of the participants completed ten introductory guided meditations on Headspace, and the other half listened to an audiobook about meditation with no guided practice.

At the end of this control period, the group who had been meditating reported they felt more positive emotions. They felt less burdened by external pressure and responsibilities than the group listening to the audiobook. These positive benefits came after just ten guided meditations, totaling only one hundred minutes over a month.[21] It did not take years of practice in a Buddhist temple.

A 2017 study from Carnegie Mellon University found that regular meditation via a mindfulness app helps reduce cortisol levels and blood pressure when exposed to stress.[22]

CRANIAL ELECTROTHERAPY STIMULATION

Prescription medications attempt to "fix" us via the use of chemicals. Our bodies contain multiple chemicals, so chemical intervention via pharmaceuticals helps in some situations. Our bodies operate both chemically and electrically. Internal electrical signals control a large part of our nervous system.

You might be familiar with a transcutaneous electrical nerve stimulation (TENS) unit. These devices are a popular way to manage pain by delivering tiny electrical impulses to the body's affected area. If you have ever visited a doctor for musculoskeletal pain, they may have placed small electrodes on the problem area to deliver this type of pain relief.

You can use a similar type of therapy for your mind. Our brains use naturally occurring electrical signals to operate. A cranial electrotherapy stimulation (CES) device delivers a microcurrent to our brain via small clips worn on the earlobes. The current is just millionths of an ampere, so it's several hundred times smaller than the current used in the TENS unit for muscle pain. Most users will not feel the CES current at all.

The CES device gently stimulates the brain to produce serotonin and melatonin while lowering cortisol levels. This stimulation assists the body's ability to move out of the sympathetic state to the parasympathetic state. Because of this, CES therapy helps treat anxiety, depression, and insomnia. In other words, it helps us calm down.

Our brains produce multiple types of waves—alpha, beta, gamma, theta, and infra-low—each with a different purpose. Our minds generate alpha waves when at rest, which are dominant during periods of quiet thought and meditation. A CES device can help our brains enter an alpha state more quickly.

I have used the CES device Alpha-STIM for the past couple of years. As the name suggests, it stimulates the alpha waves. The device has improved my ability to relax, getting me out of the sympathetic fight-or-flight mode into the parasympathetic state, as measured by my HRV scores.

The Food and Drug Administration classifies CES devices as a Class III medical device, so you will need a prescription to purchase one. There are currently eleven CES devices approved for sale within the United States. The prices are reasonable, with most under $1,000.

VIBRATION THERAPY

Soft or rough. Smooth or bumpy. Hot or cold. Our sense of touch can distinguish each of these sensations. Texture is to our skin what music is to our ears. Our sense of touch helps us understand and relate to our environment. Our skin has thousands of sensory receptors, which can calm our body and mind when correctly stimulated.

Touch triggers a self-soothing response in the human brain, reducing cortisol levels. Parents know the benefits of wrapping a blanket snuggly around their baby (swaddling) to mimic the warm and secure feeling of the womb. A snug swaddle is like the gentle pressure of a mother's touch. Babies tend to fall asleep quicker and stay asleep for more extended periods when swaddled.

Vibration is a form of touch. Think of it as touch on high speed. Some vibrations have a calm and soothing effect, and other vibrations have an energizing effect. You might experience different forms of vibration with a massage therapist. A slow and kneading motion on your shoulders might relax you, whereas a "karate chop" motion up and down your back may make you alert and energized.

Wearable devices can provide vibration stimulation to our skin to help reduce stress and improve energy, depending on the type of vibration. These devices are small, about the size of a watch, and attach to your wrist or ankle.

We know that stress activates our fight-or-flight sympathetic nervous system, leaving us on edge, distracted, and making it difficult to relax. Gentle vibrations can help stimulate our rest-and-digest parasympathetic nervous system. Over time, vibration therapy helps train our nervous system to remain in the parasympathetic state longer.

Developed by researchers at the University of Pittsburgh, I have been using the Apollo Neuro wearable vibration device for several months. The researchers conducted multiple studies with their device, showing a reduction in stress among a group of nurses, improved athletic performance, and recovery with athletes from the University of Minnesota, and symptom improvement in children and adolescents with anxiety and ADHD.

The Apollo Neuro offers several different "modes" of vibration, such as:

- Energy and Wake Up
- Social and Open
- Clear and Focused
- Rebuild and Recover
- Meditation and Mindfulness
- Relax and Unwind
- Sleep and Renew[23]

Each mode utilizes a different vibration type, with different intensity and patterns, to elicit the desired response.

I have found vibration therapy calming and quite easy to use. I wear my device on my ankle, and I will use it in the early morning for quick energy, during the day when I am trying to focus on a project, and while sleeping.

Vibration therapy devices can be purchased without a prescription at a cost of $200–$500. Although I am a fan of the Apollo, I would suggest purchasing an extended warranty with your device since, in my experience, their devices have a tendency to fail close to the expiration date of their twelve-month manufacturer's warranty.

TRACKING (PHYSICAL)

Now that you are exercising both your body and mind and balancing your sympathetic and parasympathetic nervous systems, it helps to track your progress.

One of the least expensive devices you can purchase for your health and longevity is a fitness tracker. These wearable devices are used by numerous people, from marathon runners to occasional gym-goers. Even senior citizens taking casual walks around the mall are counting their steps.

Although it might seem like everyone is wearing some sort of new tracking device today, the origin of these devices dates to the fifteenth century. Leonardo da Vinci drew plans for a machine to record the distance a Roman soldier walked—the world's first pedometer. It was large and bulky and required the soldier to pull it behind them.

The modern-day pedometer was created in 1965 in Japan by Dr. Yoshiro Hatano. He called it *manpo-kei*, which in English translates to "10,000 steps meter." His device inspired many to strive for 10,000 steps per day.

Fast forward from 1965 to 2009, when Fitbit launched its first tracker. Wearable devices could now track calories burned in addition to steps.

By 2022, wearable devices can now track an almost unlimited amount of physiological data, including heart rate, heart rate variability, respiratory rate, oxygen levels, sleep states, and more.

In a previous chapter, I cited the Whoop strap for tracking

HRV. It is essential to follow your performance over time if you hope to improve. The Whoop strap looks like a wristwatch but with no face. It does not tell time and will not distract you with notifications or buttons to push like a smartwatch. It is simply a low-profile tracker that collects an enormous amount of data. With no user interface on your wrist, you forget you are wearing it because there is nothing to "check."

What Whoop does behind the scenes is impressive. It has three sensors measuring your heart beats per minute, heart rate variability, electrodermal activity, ambient air temperature, and your speed or acceleration. It collects this data one hundred times per second, 24/7, if you are wearing the strap. For comparison purposes, the Apple Watch gathers heart rate data only every few minutes unless it detects you are in a workout.

Whoop uses your collected data to calculate a daily strain score and a daily recovery score. Your strain score is a measurement of how hard your cardiovascular system worked during the day. If you sat on the couch all day, your strain score might be mild. If you ran five miles, your strain score will be higher.

Overnight, your Whoop strap takes your strain score and reviews it against the quality of your sleep and other biometrics, such as respiratory rate, resting heart rate, and heart rate variability. The following morning, Whoop gives you a recovery score. This score lets you know how well your body recovered from the strain and stress of the previous day.

If you have a recovery score of 90 percent, you will know that your body is well positioned to work hard and take on additional strain during the day. If you have a recovery score of just 20 percent, that is a sign that perhaps you should take a day of rest.

Some athletes, or even casual exercisers, do the same workout daily. Sometimes they are not pushing themselves, so they are not getting better; other times they might be pushing themselves too hard, which also results in poor performance long term.

Athletes are supposed to "listen to their body" to determine how hard they should push themselves, but that is easier said than done. Sometimes our minds allow us to push beyond what we should be doing. If your body endures too much strain without sufficient recovery between workouts, you will end up in a recovery deficit. Your performance will not improve, and you will increase your risk of injury. The recovery score provided by the Whoop strap removes the guesswork and tells you exactly what is going on with your body.

The recovery score provides insight beyond just exercise. Suppose I see a low recovery score for a few days in a row without an apparent reason such as overreaching workout sessions. In that case, that is usually an indicator that I am fighting off some illness or virus.

Whoop has gathered data from many members who tested positive for COVID-19. Whoop found that most of those who tested positive showed elevated respiratory rates for several days before showing other symptoms. Whoop is not a medical device, and more research is needed. Still, preliminary findings suggest that an elevated respiratory rate is a good warning sign that you are fighting off a severe virus before you even know you are sick.

I have been amazed at how my body reacts to sugar, or rather, how Whoop can tell that I had too much sugar. There have been times when my recovery scores have been high all week, so I adequately balanced both strain and recovery, and then I wake up one morning with an abnormally low recovery score. Most of the time, the culprit was me indulging in a sugary dessert the night before. I don't think there is any fitness tracker that will eliminate my periodic enjoyment of ice cream. Still, if I have a strenuous workout planned the next day, I know cutting out sugar the day *before* will help my recovery score and performance. Whoop helps keep me honest.

Although I am a fan of Whoop, they have a strong competitor with the Oura ring. The Oura product is a ring instead of a strap, but they measure similar data. You should investigate both to see what works best for you.

Whoop does not have any hardware costs. They charge a subscription that ranges from $18 to $30 per month. Oura does not currently use a subscription model. The hardware cost for their ring is approximately $300.

TRACKING (PHYSIOLOGICAL)

Some people might not yet be ready for the time or financial investment required with longevity physicians. There is a company that offers insight on many of the markers longevity physicians will track at a very affordable price.

InsideTracker is a Cambridge, Massachusetts company founded by experts in aging, genetics, and biometric data from Harvard, MIT, and Tufts. They offer a comprehensive blood and DNA test that reports on forty-three blood biomarkers, including glucose, cholesterol, cortisol, and hemoglobin, for a holistic analysis of your health. Their biomarker analysis is 100 percent personalized to your data, and it is presented via a mobile app that provides daily recommendations with adjustments for your diet, exercise, and supplement regiment. Their app will also allow for uploads from certain fitness trackers such as Garmin or Fitbit.

Their plans range from $179 up to $589. You can learn more about their offerings at https://www.insidetracker.com.

Full disclosure: The author is a very small minority investor in InsideTracker but receives no compensation for sales of their testing kits/app.

IMPORTANT FDA DISCLOSURE

Although I have personally benefited from the various products and devices referenced in this book, it is important to disclose that:

These statements have not been evaluated by the Food and Drug Administration. These products are not intended to diagnose, treat, cure, or prevent any disease.

CONCLUSION

HAPPY EIGHTIETH WEDDING ANNIVERSARY

May the road rise to meet you,
May the wind be always at your back.
May the sun shine warm upon your face.
The rains fall soft upon your fields.
And until we meet again,
May God hold you in the palm of his hand.
Here's to us, and to hell with the rest of them! Cheers!

You might recognize the first part of that toast as the Irish blessing. The last line was all Tom—his sense of humor is as strong as it has ever been. He was giving a toast at a party thrown by his five children in honor of his eightieth wedding anniversary with Sarah.

What a milestone. The year is 2071, and Tom and Sarah are 105 years old.

Tom and Sarah used the *Section 16 GPS* process to amplify their wealth and accumulate assets in the first half of their lives and then used *The Healthspan Extender* mindset to focus on their physical and mental well-being and buy back their health in the second half. Their net worth at age 55 was significant enough to afford the best longevity physicians, coaches, and equipment to help make age 100 the new 70.

After a few years of focusing on his health, Tom felt like he was aging backward. He had more energy at 60 than he did at 50 and felt like he could work forever.

Tom eventually decided to retire from Silica-Corp at age 64. The CEO and board of Silica-Corp wanted him to stay longer, and they offered Tom a significant "golden handcuff" financial incentive to do so. The decision was not about money. Tom and Sarah simply had other things in the second half of their lives they wanted to accomplish. They were feeling terrific and energized, had accumulated an eight-figure net worth, and were ready for the next chapter.

As Tom and I reviewed many times over the years, "retirement" is not the end of the game—it is simply the beginning of the second half. What a fantastic second half they have played!

In the years before Tom's retirement, they funded their donor advised fund with appreciated shares of Silica-Corp stock. By the time Tom stepped down, they had accumulated over $2 million in their account to fund future charitable endeavors. Their charitable fund is now making grants to charities in the range of $75,000–$100,000 annually, while maintaining the principal value for future generations to gift. Their children and grandchildren currently direct about half of the gifts each year, and Tom and Sarah manage the rest. They are especially proud of how they passed their charitable mindset to their children and now they enjoy seeing the same values passed on to their grandchildren.

Shortly after retirement, Tom and Sarah took a volunteer trip to Africa. They worked on building a school in Kenya. They were the oldest volunteers swinging hammers, but their stamina was an inspiration to the younger volunteers. Today, their charitable fund makes an annual donation to that school to assist with operating expenses.

When they completed the school project, they stayed in Africa and took a trip to Tanzania to climb Mount Kilimanjaro at age 65. Two of their children joined them, and it was an incredible experience.

At age 70, Tom was asked to consider joining the board of a midsize private company. Someone who used to work for Tom at Silica-Corp founded the company. The board stipend was modest, but Tom received restricted stock each year.

Tom spent five years on this board, mentoring the younger executive team. His work paid off because the company ultimately went public, and Tom's restricted shares soared in value.

Sarah ended up realizing her horticulture dreams. At age 66, she set up a greenhouse in their backyard. By age 76, Tom and Sarah purchased some acreage not too far from their home, and Sarah now has eight greenhouses. She oversees the work, but most of it is tended to by volunteers from a local food pantry—her greenhouses donate all their produce to the food pantry. She has also established a special greenhouse for floriculture and donates all the flowers to local churches. Sarah still spends time most days at her "private" greenhouse at home.

Tom and Sarah still exercise regularly, and their weight training has helped them maintain bone density. In their eighties, they decided to try something new and got involved in a local pickleball league. They have slowed down a bit but are competitive in the 70-plus age group. They like winning, but that is not the point. They just want to stay active.

They also enjoy traveling regularly to see their children and grandchildren. They still take occasional trips just for themselves, but having the flexibility, financial resources, and stamina to travel to see their children is a blessing.

Most importantly, Tom and Sarah have a personal relationship with each of their ten grandchildren and twenty great-grandchildren. It is almost a full-time job keeping up with everyone. Tom and Sarah call and text regularly with the next generations and have been fortunate to attend multiple sporting events and drama productions over the years. Some of the grandchildren have become nice "travel buddies" when their parents cannot take time off.

At age 100, they welcomed their first great-*great*-grandchild into the world. There were five great-great-grandchildren in attendance at their eightieth wedding anniversary party.

As Tom finished his toast, he looked out over the guests in attendance at the party and smiled. At age 105, Tom is not sure what the rest of the "game" will bring. It feels as if he has already won the second half, but he is not yet ready to head to the locker room.

His children, grandchildren, great-grandchildren, and now great-great-grandchildren give Tom and Sarah relationships they value every day. Plus, they are having a great time at this party. Would it not be amazing to do it all over again in five years?

Tom raised his glass one more time, but this time he smiled and made a silent toast.

Here's hoping our game will head into overtime. Cheers.

ACKNOWLEDGMENTS

Writing *Section 16 Secrets* was significantly more difficult and time-consuming than I ever imagined. I started this journey three years ago, in January 2020, when I first met with the publishing team in Austin. At the time, I thought the process would take six months, not three years.

There are many people I would like to thank for their assistance on this journey. Some people have improved my personal life, some have improved my business life, and many have touched both. Without the support of these individuals, this book would have remained in my head and not in your hands.

Thank you, Donna. What an amazing run we've had over the past twenty-nine years. It's exciting to think we are not yet halfway to our eightieth anniversary. Thank you for putting up with me running off to my scheduled writing sessions each morning. The best thing that ever happened to me was meeting you on September 5, 1988.

Thank you, Billy. As our oldest son, there was always a lot of pressure on you as the "trailblazer." You provided your mother and me with a lot of firsts. From preschool, to college, to athletics, to AP tests, and then your wedding, we learned alongside you, which benefited all your siblings. Now that you are an adult, I am so proud of the different business ventures you have started and your success with your current company. You seem to balance everything so well. You live up to your high "quick start" score in your Kolbe profile.

Thank you, Matthew. Coaching your basketball team was one of the highlights of my first fifty trips around the sun. The résumé you built during college was impressive, and that hard work paid off with your wealth management career in New York City. Whenever I lose focus on my daily health goals, all I have to do is take a look at your Whoop strain score, and that pushes me to work just a little bit harder. Health needs to be my focus for the *next* fifty trips around the sun, and your dedication benefits both of us.

Thank you, Nathan. Being the father of a collegiate baseball pitcher is pretty stressful. I think my heart would beat faster than yours when you would take the field with bases loaded. I continue to be amazed at how calm, cool, and collected you were on the mound, and I love seeing that demeanor carry over into your business career. You are one of the most even-keeled people I have ever met, which will serve you well in life. You are also the only person I know who can juggle while riding a unicycle. I am proud to have witnessed all your talents from the front row.

Thank you, Catherine. I still remember one of your "athlete

of the week" interviews when the TV reporter asked how you could balance being a three-sport athlete while taking a full course load. You responded that it was easier to keep up with school while you were in-season because you had to rely on time management—you were wise beyond your years. You have always been so busy with your various jobs, internships, and freelance work, and yet everything gets done. You have cracked that code and are an inspiration to all of us. Your sense of humor is also off the charts. Please utilize *Section 16 Secrets* as the official acknowledgment that I do indeed consider you the funniest Burns child.

Thank you, Braeden. I remember a time when I was coaching your sixth-grade basketball team and you said something so funny and insightful during practice that I turned and said, "You know, Braeden, I would dig hanging out with you even if you weren't my son." I still feel that way today. You are one of the most caring and thoughtful humans I have ever met, and I can't wait to see what life has in store for you and then reminisce about all of it at your fiftieth high school jubilee celebration.

Thank you, Shannon. I love you like you were my biological child. We were all so happy when Billy brought you into our family. I am so excited for the life the two of you will share. The fact that Catherine told me, "Shannon is your best shot at getting D-1 grandchildren," is just a side benefit.

Thank you, Mr. and Mrs. Barnaba. Our son Billy said it best a few years ago: "I really miss Grandpa, but Mr. B. has done a great job filling in." Seeing the love that Gary and Sheila share is an inspiration to Donna and me. Not just your love for each other but your love for *everyone* less fortunate. The number of kids you have helped in our community over the years is astounding, and most people have no idea what you've done.

Thank you, Nick and Jill Murphy at Mission Fitness. I still remember when I met Nick in May 2017—he asked me how much weight I wanted to lose, I said one hundred pounds, and he quickly shrugged that off and said, "Oh, that's nothing." Since that didn't scare him off, I upped it to 124 pounds to get me down to 185. I hit that weight 294 days later. Thank you both for your friendship and continued guidance on my journey.

Thank you to Bill, Kelley, and Chris at Burns Matteson Capital Management and their spouses Patti, Andrew, and Kerri. You kept the ship sailing when I needed to come in late each morning after my writing sessions. I am so fortunate to be able to work with you daily.

Thank you to everyone at Strategic Coach. Without the mentorship of Dan Sullivan and Babs Smith, I would never have written *Section 16 Secrets*. Dan taught me the benefit of breaking things down into ninety-day jumps and having a twenty-five-year plan. So many people at Strategic Coach have inspired me that it is tough to remember them all. But here goes: Thank you, Shannon, Nicole, Kristi, Teresa, Katelyn, Meghann, Cathy, Julia, Marilyn, Becca, Serafina, Arianna, Jill, Alex, Carolyn, Ted, Franco, Justin, Mark B., Mark N., Leslie, Ingrid, Michael (MZ), Kate, and all of the other entrepreneurs I've had the pleasure of working with. You rock.

Thank you to Dr. Jeffery Gladden and Dr. Ernie Navarro and the team at Gladden Longevity. Jeff, Ernie, Katie, Jaylin, Haley, Grace, Holly, Melissa, and Christina are all valued partners in my journey to age 105 (and hopefully beyond). I am honored to be a part of Jeff's goal to see humans push themselves beyond age 120.

Thank you, Shawn Tolleson and Tolleson Health Advisers. It was your encouragement that prompted me to compete in my very first Spartan race at age 50. Thank you for making that an attainable goal.

Thank you to my Syracuse Nets Teams. One of the things that keeps you young is hanging out with younger people. As a business owner, it is easy to find yourself working nonstop seven days a week. You guys made it possible for me to step away from "work" and focus on something that was "fun." Traveling across the country with you has been one of the highlights of my life. I have fond memories of the actual games, but my most treasured memories are the hotels, car rides, plane trips, and restaurants with each of you. Thank you, Matt, Isaiah, Caleb, Jordan, Jake, Zach, David, James, and all the guys. I am excited to see what life has in store for each of you.

Thank you, Bofa Deez, for always making my children laugh.

Thank you, James Dodge at Commit Action. Our Monday calls kept me on track throughout this project. Your encouragement and support moved me forward each week.

Thank you to Tucker Max and everyone at Scribe Media and Lioncrest Publishing. I still cannot believe you got this book out of me. Thank you, Emily, Hal, Esty, Aleza, Lisa, Skyler, Erin, Rebecca, Joy, Candace, Caroline, and the entire team.

Thank you to the legal department and executive benefits group at Corning Inc. We work with many companies, and the Corning crew is the best of the best. Thank you for putting up with all my questions to assist our clients. Special thanks to Linda J., Linda H., Lewis, John, Kevyn, and Dan who have the quickest response time of any professionals in the nation.

Thank you to all our friends and clients across twenty-four states whom I cannot name personally. It has been an honor serving you over the past two-plus decades. I am most proud of getting to see your children grow and mature and playing a small part in helping you pass your positive mindset on to the next generation.

ABOUT THE AUTHOR

WILLIAM BURNS is the founder of Burns Matteson Capital Management, an SEC Registered Investment Advisory firm with clients in twenty-four states. He is a CERTIFIED FINANCIAL PLANNER™ professional, health and longevity enthusiast, author, and speaker.

He assists Section 16 corporate executives and other high-networth families reclaim time from their busy lives, providing peace of mind as an independent counsel for complex financial matters.

He enjoys exploring the science of health and longevity and has the aggressive but obtainable goal of living to age 105 and forging meaningful relationships with his great-grandchildren.

He and his wife, Donna, have been blessed with five children and live in Upstate New York.

NOTES

1   Vivek Wadhwa, Richard B. Freeman, and Ben A. Rissing, *Education and Tech Entrepreneurship* (Kansas City: Ewing Marion Kauffman Foundation, 2008), http://dx.doi.org/10.2139/ssrn.1127248.

2   "Want to Live Longer and Better? Do Strength Training," *Harvard Business Review*, February 15, 2021, https://www.health.harvard.edu/staying-healthy/want-to-live-longer-and-better-do-strength-training.

3   Jennifer Abbasi, "Strength Training Helps Older Adults Live Longer," Penn State, April 20, 2016, https://www.psu.edu/news/research/story/strength-training-helps-older-adults-live-longer/.

4   Carlos A. Celis-Morales et al., "Associations of Grip Strengths with Cardiovascular, Respiratory, and Cancer Outcomes and All Cause Mortality: Prospective Cohort Study of Half a Million UK Biobank Participants," *BMJ* 361, no. k1651 (2018), https://doi.org/10.1136/bmj.k1651.

5   Darryl P. Leong et al., "Prognostic Value of Grip Strength: Findings from the Prospective Urban Rural Epidemiology (PURE) Study," *The Lancet* 386, no. 9990 (2015): 266–273, https://doi.org/10.1016/S0140-6736(14)62000-6.

6   Daniel K. Mroczek and Avron Spiro, "Personality Change Influences Mortality in Older Men," *Psychological Science* 18, no. 5 (2007), https://doi.org/10.1111/j.1467-9280.2007.01907.x

7   E. Patterson et al., "Health Implications of High Dietary Omega-6 Polyunsaturated Fatty Acids," *Journal of Nutrition and Metabolism* 2012, no. 539426 (2012), https://doi.org/10.1155/2012/539426.

8   "Fasting Increases Health and Lifespan in Male Mice," *NIH Research Matters*,
    September 18, 2018, https://www.nih.gov/news-events/nih-research-matters/
    fasting-increases-health-lifespan-male-mice.

9   Valter D. Longo et al., "Intermittent and Periodic Fasting, Longevity and Disease," *Nature
    Aging* 1 (2021): 47–59, https://doi.org/10.1038/s43587-020-00013-3.

10 Robert Perkins, "Diet that Mimics Fasting Appears to Slow Aging," USC News, June 18,
    2015, https://news.usc.edu/82959/diet-that-mimics-fasting-appears-to-slow-aging/.

11 Soo-Jin Oh, Jae Kyung Lee, and Ok Sarah Shin, "Aging and the Immune System: The
    Impact of Immunosenescence on Viral Infection, Immunity and Vaccine Immunogenicity,"
    Immune Network 19, no. 6 (2019), https://doi.org/10.4110/in.2019.19.e37.

12 Mario Falchi et al., "Low Copy Number of the Salivary Amylase Gene Predisposes to
    Obesity," *Nature Genetics* 46 (2014): 492–497, https://doi.org/10.1038/ng.2939.

13 Karen Hamrick, "Americans Spend an Average of 37 Minutes a Day Preparing and
    Serving Food and Cleaning Up," USDA, November 7, 2016, https://www.ers.usda.gov/
    amber-waves/2016/november/americans-spend-an-average-of-37-minutes-a-day-
    preparing-and-serving-food-and-cleaning-up/.

14 Tanjaniina Laukkanen et al., "Association Between Sauna Bathing and Fatal
    Cardiovascular and All-Cause Mortality Events," *JAMA Intern Mededicine* 175, no. 4
    (2015): 542–548, http://dx.doi.org/10.1001/jamainternmed.2014.8187.

15 Beat Knechtle et al., "Cold Water Swimming—Benefits and Risks: A Narrative Review,"
    International Journal of Environmental Research and Public Health 17, no. 23 (2020),
    https://doi.org/10.3390/ijerph17238984.

16 Brandon C. Irwin et al., "Aerobic Exercise Is Promoted When Individual Performance
    Affects the Group: A Test of the Kohler Motivation Gain Effect," *Annals of Behavioral
    Medicine* 44, no. 2 (2012): 151–159, https://doi.org/10.1007/s12160-012-9367-4.

17 Kansas State University, "Burning More Calories Is Easier When
    Working Out with Someone You Perceive as Better," research results,
    Newswise, November 26, 2012, https://www.newswise.com/articles/
    burning-more-calories-is-easier-when-working-out-with-someone-you-perceive-as-better.

18 Kazue Okamoto-Mizuno and Koh Mizuno, "Effects of Thermal Environment on Sleep
    and Circadian Rhythm," *Journal of Physiological Anthropology* 31, no. 14 (2012), https://doi.
    org/10.1186/1880-6805-31-14.

19 Carol Torgan, "Cool Temperature Alters Human Fat and Metabolism," *NIH Research
    Matters*, July 28, 2014, https://www.nih.gov/news-events/nih-research-matters/
    cool-temperature-alters-human-fat-metabolism.

20 Justin S. Feinstein et al., "Examining the Short-Term Anxiolytic and Antidepressant Effect of Floatation-REST," *PLoS ONE* 13, no. 2 (2018), https://doi.org/10.1371/journal.pone.0190292.

21 Marcos Economides et al., "Improvements in Stress, Affect, and Irritability Following Brief Use of a Mindfulness-Based Smartphone App: A Randomized Controlled Trial," *Mindfulness* 9 (2018): 1584–1593, https://doi.org/10.1007/s12671-018-0905-4.

22 Emily K. Lindsay et al., "Acceptance Lowers Stress Reactivity: Dismantling Mindfulness Training in a Randomized Controlled Trial," *Psychoneuroendocrinology* 87 (2018): 63–73, https://doi.org/10.1016/j.psyneuen.2017.09.015.

23 "Apollo Neuro Research: Read the Research Behind the Results," Apollo Neuro, accessed September 13, 2022, https://apolloneuro.com/pages/studies-roundup.

Made in United States
North Haven, CT
26 July 2023